Persuading the Public

The Evolution of Popular Presidential Communication from Washington to Trump

ANNE C. PLUTA

UNIVERSITY PRESS OF KANSAS

To my mother

Published by the University Press of Kansas (Lawrence, Kansas 66045),
which was organized by the Kansas Board of Regents and is operated
and funded by Emporia State University, Fort Hays State University,
Kansas State University, Pittsburg State University, the University of Kansas,
and Wichita State University.

Library of Congress Cataloging-in-Publication Data

Names: Pluta, Anne C., author.
Title: Persuading the public : the evolution of popular presidential
communication from Washington to Trump / Anne C. Pluta.
Description: Lawrence : University Press of Kansas, 2023. | Includes
bibliographical references and index.
Identifiers: LCCN 2022034709 (print) | LCCN 2022034710 (ebook)
ISBN 9780700635368 (cloth)
ISBN 9780700634347 (paperback)
ISBN 9780700634354 (ebook)
Subjects: LCSH: Communication in politics—United States—History. |
Political oratory—United States—History. | Presidents—United
States—Language—History. | Mass media—Political aspects—United
States—History.
Classification: LCC JA85.2.U6 P59 2023 (print) | LCC JA85.2.U6 (ebook) |
DDC 302.230973—dc23/eng/20230103
LC record available at https://lccn.loc.gov/2022034709.
LC ebook record available at https://lccn.loc.gov/2022034710.

British Library Cataloguing-in-Publication Data is available.

Printed in the United States of America

10 9 8 7 6 5 4 3 2 1

The paper used in this publication is acid free and meets the minimum
requirements of the American National Standard for Permanence of Paper
for Printed Library Materials Z39.48-1992.a

Contents

Acknowledgments

I have been working on this book for more than a decade. It began to take shape when I was a graduate student at the University of California–Santa Barbara (UCSB), where I completed an independent study project on the presidency with John Woolley. I had long been fascinated by history, and an exploration of the presidency almost always has history at its core. I had a number of great teachers at UCSB. Among them, Kent Jennings and Heather Stoll patiently taught me methodology, slowly shaping this historian into a political scientist. Kate Bruhn and Stephen Weatherford asked gentle but pointed questions that made everything I did better. But my greatest debt is to John Woolley. We shared a passion for the presidency, and he allowed me to lean into the history while still insisting on rigorous social science. Most important, he continued to provide guidance and wisdom long after his obligation ended, and I continued to be very grateful. Of course, no graduate school experience is complete without fellow students, and though time and distance have taken their toll, I will always remember Jeanette Harvey, Marcus Arraj, E. G. Garay, Emiliana Patlan, and Michael Albert with fondness for their friendship during our time at UCSB.

I met Julia Azari while I was still a student. She took me under her wing and showed me the ropes. The last ten years of APSA and MPSA have been much richer because of our friendship. I am grateful to David Congdon, who believed in this project when few others did. I thank him for allowing me to work through early drafts and eventually find the right structure.

My colleagues at Rowan have provided support and an academic community for the last seven years. Lawrence Markowitz spent a lot of time talking with me about presidents and American political development, even though both topics are far from his area of interest. Misty Knight-Finley is an amazing colleague and a better friend.

Finally, nothing I have accomplished would be possible without the support of my family: my parents, John and Christina, who worked hard to give me every opportunity; my brothers, John and Andrew, and especially my sister Larissa, who carefully read and edited an early draft of the book; my aunts, Patricia and Larissa; my uncle, Myron; my cousins and their children (Olesh, Jessica, Roman, Christian, Lada, Theodorous, Nikolas, Lida, Maria, Evhen, Nicole, and Julian), who are a valuable source of fun whenever writing becomes too tedious; Sarah, who can always bring a smile to my face with her warmth and silliness; and last, but of course not least, Adam, who has pushed me, supported me, and loved me through it all.

Introduction

In the twenty-first century, the power and ubiquity of the American president are well documented in newspapers, movies, and books. In fact, it is not uncommon to hear the president referred to as the most powerful person on earth. How and to what end presidents wield this power is a subject of great interest and debate among scholars from a number of disciplines, journalists, and the public at large. One area of study is presidential communication strategies. Presidents can move economic markets, rally supporters, chasten opponents, and comfort the public with their words. Similarly, poor rhetorical leadership can have consequences, leaving the nation rudderless and without direction at critical moments.

The visibility of the president and the ever-present nature of his words are taken for granted today, and although there are some towering figures from the past—George Washington, Thomas Jefferson, Abraham Lincoln, and Theodore Roosevelt—there is also a common assumption that earlier presidents were aloof and removed from politics. In fact, there are many examples of early presidents working to connect directly with the American people. For practical reasons (which I discuss at length), these kinds of presidential communications were less frequent than they are today, but they offer a window into the development of the American political landscape. Examples of what I call popular presidential communications from the eighteenth and nineteenth centuries include George Washington visiting all thirteen states in an effort to solidify the tenuous bonds of the new nation and Andrew Jackson's extensive messages to the public on contentious issues such as the National Bank and nullification. Even underestimated presidents like Rutherford B. Hayes, Benjamin

Harrison, and William Taft traveled across the country and spoke to the American people to advance their political agendas.

Presidential speech is now seen as commonplace and routine, and presidents carefully calculate their rhetorical strategies, reluctant to cede any potential advantage to their opponents. Throughout history, presidents have sought to cut out intermediaries and reach the public as directly as possible, signaling the importance of this relationship. Ronald Reagan's and Barack Obama's successes are linked to their ability to capture the public's attention through the latest advances in communications technology. Now, former president Donald Trump's use of Twitter has threatened to upend our understanding of presidential communication, and his ability to reach his supporters directly esulted in a crisis of democracy.

The Argument

The core argument of this book is that structural factors shape opportunities for political communication, something I call opportunistic communication. In the case of American presidents, this relationship works in three ways. First, the media environment creates the president's audience by shaping who the president has the ability to persuade.[1] Second, technological innovation creates opportunities for the president to reach the public and results in changes in communication strategies. Conversely, technological limitations can impede the president's ability to reach the public. Third, the structure of political parties can either constrain or enhance the president's desire to speak on policy issues. Moreover, the nationalization of the party system has given the president greater visibility and importance. What I show in this book is that presidents know their relationship to the public is unique in the political arena, and they have sought opportunities to leverage this connection throughout history. However, especially in the late eighteenth and early nineteenth centuries, there was a significant cost associated with reaching out to the public because of limited technology, a partisan media environment, and strong parties. Despite these constraints, even early presidents went to the people, although not with the same frequency as their successors, who encountered fewer barriers.

I find that throughout history, presidents have operated in an inherently competitive environment where they are forced to adjust not only to their opponents but also to technological innovations, an ever-evolving relationship with their party, the growth and transformation of the American electorate, and a changing media environment. These forces have had a remarkably consistent influence on presidential communication strategies, despite taking various forms throughout history. As these opportunity structures change, so does the president's method of communicating.

With this argument in mind, I provide a comprehensive catalog of the evolution of popular presidential communication from George Washington through Donald Trump.[2] While the content of these two presidents' rhetoric could not be more different, similar structural factors scaffold the relationship between the president and the people. For example, the best historical analogy to understanding Trump comes from Andrew Johnson. An outsider with little commitment to the Republican Party, Johnson felt eternally aggrieved and engaged in rhetorical outbursts that earned him widespread recriminations. Similarly, many of the driving factors I examine, including a diffuse and partisan media environment and a high degree of polarization, were present in both the 1860s and the 2010s.

I am hardly the first scholar to see the importance of popular presidential communication or to study its evolution. One of the most enduring works is Jeffrey Tulis's *The Rhetorical Presidency* (1987). Tulis categorizes the rhetorical behavior of nineteenth-century presidents as only ceremonial and exceedingly rare. In fact, he hypothesizes that a constitutional norm prevented presidents from discussing policy positions with the public. This argument quickly gained purchase but was also challenged in ways that were theoretically sound and methodologically varied. For the most part, however, these works focused on specific presidents, particular aspects of rhetoric, or a limited period of time. Mel Laracey's *Presidents and the People* (2002), one of the most important rebuttals to Tulis, covers the same period: from Washington to McKinley. Others, such as edited volumes by Richard Ellis (1998) and Martin Medhurst (2008), offer chapters by different scholars on selected presidents. Another book by Ellis (2008) is remarkable because it covers the entirety of the institution but focuses on presidential travel (a vital aspect of popular presidential communication that I address in detail). Despite the significant amount of scholarship challenging Tulis, his work remains widely cited, in part because there is no clear theoretical alternative.[3] In this book I offer the concept of opportunistic communication to explain the relationship between the president and the people within a framework of opportunities structured by technology, the media environment, enfranchisement, and party politics—not constitutional norms. I bring new empirical evidence to bear and advance a novel theoretical approach to understanding the development of presidential rhetoric. I also synthesize a broad and sometimes divergent literature that spans many decades and multiple disciplines to provide a comprehensive account of presidential rhetoric.

The new evidence I utilize shows that early presidents provided an important foundation on which their successors built and continue to build their rhetorical strategies. I find little support for a constitutional norm prohibiting presidents from addressing the public, particularly in the cases of Thomas Jefferson and Woodrow Wilson, where this kind of norm violation would be most apparent and therefore most likely to produce a backlash. Using newly digitized newspaper sources, I compiled a unique data set of presidential public speech from 1789 to 2021. My data set not only replicates those examples in Tulis's landmark book but also includes additional speeches and remarks. I found at least 40 percent more examples of early (Washington through McKinley) presidential speech than Tulis reported. I am not the first to encounter many of these communications, but because of their obscurity and, until recently, inaccessibility, they are unknown to many scholars.[4] Therefore, many of these remarks have never been systematically cataloged and counted, as I do here. In addition, I have recorded details such as where the speech was given, the audience, and the content. In combining these data with those from the American Presidency Project, I am able to offer a unique and comprehensive view of presidential rhetoric from 1789 to 2021.[5]

Finally, I provide insight into changes in American politics through the lens of popular presidential communication, ranging from the earliest presidents' efforts to solidify a tenuous federal union to later presidents' attempts to hold together (or not) a large and increasingly diverse polity. I offer accounts from historical newspapers that shed new light on how presidential communication was understood by both elites and the general public. These views are important because they allow us to put presidential rhetoric in the context of its time rather than apply a contemporary lens to the past.

At the same time, I synthesize a massive field of research and provide analytical order to the conversation. Research on presidential communication can be found not only in the disciplines of political science and communication but also in history and rhetorical studies. Journalists provide another rich trove of information. I bring order to this vast multidisciplinary literature by analyzing presidential speech using four dimensions: mode (spoken or written), frequency (how often presidents speak), content (what they talk about), and audience (who they are speaking to). By tracing the entirety of the history, I offer a unique account of popular presidential communication and provide novel insights and a comprehensive theoretical approach to explain its development.

Presidential Rhetoric and American Democracy

Despite being controversial and vague at its inception, the presidency quickly grew into an essential aspect of American democracy because of the president's distinct relationship with the public. This relationship is forged by three institutional and constitutional incentives: the president's desire to cultivate a national identity, the need to build legitimacy, and the president's relative weakness in the legislative process. I discuss these factors at length.

Though not the intention of all the founders, the presidency as established in the Constitution creates three incentives for the president to communicate and have a relationship with the people. First, the president is both the head of state and the head of government. As the head of state, the president has an incentive, if not a duty, to cultivate an identity for the nation. This essential task is difficult in part because of the elusive nature of national identity. As famously defined by Benedict Anderson (2006), nations are "imagined communities" that need to be continuously created and re-created by political elites. National identity is the symbolic elaboration of this imagined community (Spillman 1997, 3). And creating and maintaining an identity for the nation depend on a connection with the public. National identity is particularly complex in the United States, given the diversity of a population composed largely of immigrants (Beasley 2004).

Second, the very nature of democracy means that the president derives his legitimacy from the people (Genovese 2006). Legitimacy is a complex concept that can be simplified to mean public acceptance of or acquiescence to leadership. For American presidents, legitimacy is a "link between prestige and formal powers" and is not based only on constitutionally afforded powers (Neustadt [1960] 1991, 165; Anderson 1988). The view that legitimacy is derived from the public can be traced to John Locke's notion of the consent of the governed, an idea on which much of the Constitution is based (Lupel 2001, 307). Legitimacy can be especially complicated for American presidents in two situations: those who lose the popular vote yet win in the Electoral College, and those who become accidental presidents. In both cases, presidents cannot claim to be the choice of the majority, though some are likely to say they have a mandate, regardless of this reality (Azari 2014). But even absent this electoral complication, the president's relationship to the public is an important source of power and legitimacy.

Third, the president's formal weakness in the legislative process relative to Congress necessitates a relationship with the public (Cornwall 1979, 3; Nichols 1994). In this relationship with Congress, the "ambiguity of executive power creates incentives for presidents to be dynamic and forceful agents of change" (Galvin and Shogun 2004, 477). Constitutionally, a president's power to legislate is limited to the veto and an annual message in which he can make his legislative priorities known. However, expectations of the presidency, even in the earliest days of an administration, are often much greater. The president represents the sole elected official who can claim to speak for the American people as a whole. The president must also maintain party unity and discipline in the legislative process (Gamm and Smith 1998; Korzi 2004; Klinghard 2010). All these roles require rhetorical leadership.

Rhetorical leadership is essential to the institution and has been so since the founding. Presidents since George Washington have worked to build and enhance the connection between the executive and the public. However, the president operates in a complex political environment that is ever changing and inherently competitive. This relationship has evolved in response to numerous factors, such as innovations in communication and travel technologies, the development of political parties, the expansion of the electoral franchise, and a changing media environment. The electorate has grown dramatically over the last 250 years, vastly increasing the number of people and interests the president represents and speaks to. Technological innovation, an evolving media environment, and political incentives affect how presidents communicate with the public and account for the changing nature of presidential rhetoric. Because presidential communication with the public is a fundamental feature of American democracy, understanding its progress is central to unpacking how and why American politics changes.

The Persuadable Public

In 1960 Richard Neustadt famously wrote that the power of the presidency is the power to persuade. In his view, the only way for the president to navigate the complexities and inherent inertia of American government is through bargaining and influence. Today, presidents speak frequently to the American public, despite scholarly disagreement about the effectiveness of this rhetoric (G. Edwards 2006; G. C. Edwards 2007; Eshbaugh-Soha 2015). This concern about the president's ability to influence the public is somewhat recent and is in some ways a product of a diverse and fragmented media environment that makes reaching the people difficult (Baum and Kernell 1999, 2006; Baum 2011).

The president is, by the very nature of the institution, always speaking to the nation and often claims to speak for the American public as a whole (Ragsdale 1987). However, the public as a whole is not always persuadable for three reasons: First, throughout much of American history, large swaths of the population were disenfranchised. Second, the president may be unable to reach the public as a whole because of the nature of the media environment—interestingly, this has been the case for a majority of American history. Third, partisanship and polarization make many Americans unpersuadable, despite the president's best efforts. There have been a few exceptional moments in history when presidents were able to reach and persuade the public as a whole, but these moments are aberrations. In fact, for most of American history, presidents have been aware that wholesale persuasion is exceedingly difficult and have focused their efforts on those parts of the public they can mobilize. In my estimation, the evolution of popular presidential communication is structured by the persuadable public, or those citizens who can participate in the electoral system, who the president can reach, and who are open to having their minds changed.

As I will show, presidents expend considerable resources in communicating with the public. They direct their energies toward not only the content of their rhetoric but also how the speech is delivered and who is most likely to hear it. Why do presidents do this? Wouldn't their energies be better spent on Capitol Hill or in talks with world leaders? As I explore throughout this book, the public is an important perceived locus of power for American presidents, and it is critical that they cultivate this relationship to achieve political goals, including their own reelection, the election of partisans, and the implementation of policy priorities. The president's communication involves another strategic element: being heard over the opposition, especially when the barriers to entry are low (as in today's media environment). If the president is quiet, then his opponents are likely framing the terms of political debate, with potentially disastrous consequences for the chief executive.

The Rise of the "Rhetorical Presidency" and "Going Public"

Understanding the nature and causes of change in presidential rhetoric has been an important part of political science research for the better part of the last four decades. Ceaser et al. (1981) introduced the term "rhetorical presidency" to describe the public communication strategy of the American president. Tulis (1987) further explored the topic in his work *The Rhetorical Presidency*. Both suggested that increased public speaking by American presidents was problematic because it precluded democratic deliberation and encouraged demagoguery.[6] During the same time, Samuel Kernell ([1986] 1997) introduced the concept of "going public" to describe the process by which the president of the United States takes his message to the people to circumvent the bargaining process in Washington. In sum, these arguments view early presidents as reserved stewards of the executive branch, as opposed to active participants in policy debate.

Together, Kernell's and Tulis's works set the stage for a research agenda that endures, including rebuttals (Ellis 1998, 2008; Laracey 2002; Medhurst 2008; Hoffman 2010; Pluta 2015) and extensions (Lim 2008). Moreover, Tulis and other scholars (Lim 2008; Zug 2018, 2019) continue to dismiss alternative accounts of early presidential rhetoric, instead pressing the idea that Woodrow Wilson ushered in what amounts to a constitutional change in his approach to communicating with the public. While I concede that much has changed in the rhetorical content and character of American presidents, I find this evolution rooted in external forces and institutional incentives rather than individual assessments of the constitutionally appropriate role of the chief executive.

Drawing Lines

A central part of my argument is that although rhetorical leadership has been part of the presidency since its inception, popular presidential communication has evolved over time in response to exogenous forces. This evolution has been layered and has involved learning, which leads me to approach the study of presidential communication strategy in very broad terms.[7]

Understandably, presidency scholars often look for clear inflection or break points. They do this in part because of the availability of data. Speeches post Herbert Hoover have been systematically collected and are easy to access through sources such as the American Presidency Project. In addition, Wilson's innovative approach to the annual message (later called the State of the Union address) and Franklin D. Roosevelt's masterful use of the radio provide clear examples of what seem to be breaks from the past. Although these are certainly important events, they are most usefully understood in the broader context of the institution.

My outlook on popular presidential communication is similar to that of the many scholars who criticize the modern-traditional divide as being too simplistic (Teten 2003, 2008; Nichols 1994; Bimes and Mulroy 2004) or others who conceptualize a slow development of the institution and caution against treating the nineteenth-century presidency as a single static type (Bimes 2009; Ellis 1998; Medhurst 2008; Greenstein 2009). My approach suggests that early presidents are just as important as later ones, if not more so, given that they are often overlooked by scholars and that these early communication practices can shed light on recent developments.

However, a project this large needs to be organized in some way. With this in mind, I have created audience eras to structure my argument. I acknowledge that the lines between them are fuzzy and some aspects of each category bleed into others because political change is often slow. I consider the persuadable public typology as a guide rather than a definitive interpretation of each presidency. I begin with the earliest presidents, in an era I call "going elite." These presidents focused their communications on national and local elites. Given that mass-based parties and political participation were in their infancy, this approach made sense. Andrew Jackson's election, the strengthening of the party system, and the improvement of printing technologies allowed presidents to address their partisans through the administration newspaper, leading to the "going partisan" approach. The railroad and post–Civil War concerns encouraged presidents to "go regional." Expansion of the railroad, the lessening of sectional tensions, and the growth of pluralism led presidents to start to seek a national audience (often through the press). I call this "going almost national" because technological constraints prevented presidents from addressing the whole nation simultaneously. The invention of radio and later television created a truly national audience, so I call this period "going national." Finally, a discursive media environment and growing polarization led presidents to address local, specific, and often partisan audiences, an approach I call "going targeted." Table I.1 summarizes the persuadable public across time and the institutional factors that structure it.

Dimensions of Popular Presidential Communication

One of my argument's core theoretical contributions is the development of the dimensions of popular presidential communication. This analytical framework brings much-needed consistency and structure to

Table I.1: The Persuadable Public by Era

Presidents (Years)	Era	Public	Parties/ Partisanship	Media, Communication, and Travel Environments
Washington–J. Q. Adams (1789–1828)	Going Elite	Elites	• Nascent parties	**Newspapers** • Administration newspaper begins, 1800 • High entry cost • High distribution cost • Travel dangerous and slow
Jackson–Lincoln (1829–1865)	Going Partisan	All white men; elites still very important (literacy)	• Mass-based parties • Strong parties (intraparty contention over slavery dilutes some strength)	**Newspapers** • Steam and rotary press invented, 1830s • Birth of Associated Press, 1848 • High entry cost; lower distribution cost • Travel slightly faster and less dangerous • End of administration newspapers, 1861
A. Johnson–B. Harrison (1866–1893)	Going Regional	All men for a short time	• Strong parties • Reconstruction • Closely contested elections	**Newspapers, Railroads** • Transcontinental railroad completed, 1869 • High entry cost • Easy to distribute • Travel much faster and less dangerous • First national tour, 1883

Era				
Cleveland–Wilson (1894–1921)	Going Almost National	Rise of interest groups	• Weakening parties	Newspapers; Railroads, Cars • First presidential travel outside US, 1906 • High entry cost; high distribution cost • More "noise" (other interests besides politics)
Harding–G. H. W. Bush (1922–1992)	Going National	Universal suffrage in name but not in practice	• Weak parties • Low polarization • Rising international power	Newspapers, Radio, TV; Railroads, Cars, Air Travel • First inaugural address broadcast on radio, 1925 • First inaugural address televised, 1949 • Boeing jet commissioned as Air Force One, 1962 • National: high entry cost; high distribution cost • Norm of objectivity • CNN begins broadcasting, 1980
Clinton–Trump (1993–2021)	Going Targeted	Universal suffrage	• Weak parties • Strong partisanship/polarization	Newspapers, Radio, TV, Cable, Internet; Railroads, Cars, Air Travel • Facebook founded, 2004 • First presidential tweet, 2015

the scholarly debate surrounding the nature of presidential rhetoric. As noted earlier, this literature is vast, speaks to various aspects of presidential communication, and does not always directly engage with itself. In particular, these dimensions make it easier to see how and why communication strategies changed. My approach allows a systematic analysis over time, but within conceptual boundaries.

I argue that presidents have always sought a relationship with the American public, but outside forces have changed how that message is delivered (mode), to whom it is delivered (audience), how often presidents speak (frequency), and what they speak about (content). These dimensions serve as the dependent variables in my analysis; however, they are not wholly independent of one another. For example, the railroad, a critical technological innovation, affected the mode (more spoken than written), the frequency (more often), and the audience (more popular) of presidential communication.

This systematic understanding of the nature of presidential rhetoric over time will lead to a more complete understanding of the development of American institutions more broadly. By analyzing the evolution of popular presidential communication along these four analytical dimensions, I bring clarity to the debate regarding the nature and purpose of presidential rhetoric throughout the history of the republic. I use these dimensions to organize my data and to show that institutional development is the result of responses to both outside pressures and outside incentives.

Methodology and Approach

Each chapter confronts the question of who is persuadable. By considering the media environment, the available technology, and political circumstances, I examine the president's audience. I argue that by considering the specific targets of presidential rhetoric, scholars can better judge its effectiveness. My approach to this analysis is twofold. I provide a descriptive account of the evolution of popular presidential communication along my four dimensions: mode, audience, frequency, and content. There is also an explanatory aspect to my analysis. I show how innovation in communication and transportation technology; political incentives, including the evolution of political parties and the expansion of voting rights; and fluctuations in the media environment caused these changes.

Although descriptive analysis is often relegated to secondary status in political science, it has important purposes. To identify causal mechanisms, one must first determine that change has occurred, as well as how and where it occurred. The dimensions of popular presidential communication require both description and explanation. Because the corpus of popular presidential rhetoric has not been compiled, the first step is to describe changes.

I used a mixed-methods approach to understanding differences in presidential rhetoric across the institution of the presidency and along each dimension of popular communication. I utilized an original data set of more than three thousand instances of pre-1929 presidential rhetoric. The collection and coding of these data are explained in the next section. I combined these data with speeches and remarks from the American Presidency Project to create a corpus of presidential rhetoric from 1789 to 2021. These data allowed a quantitative analysis of presidential speech that I used to describe the dimensions of popular communication over time where possible.

In addition, I used case studies of some presidents to illustrate broader points or to challenge conventional scholarly wisdom. These cases include George Washington's and John Adams's attempts to lead public opinion, Andrew Jackson's campaign against the National Bank, William H. Taft's surprisingly frequent rhetoric, Woodrow Wilson's precedent-shattering 1913 special message to Congress, Franklin D. Roosevelt's use of the radio to speak to a national audience, Barack Obama's application of new media to reach specific constituencies, and Donald Trump's use of interviews for targeted audiences. These case studies rely on new evidence from historical newspapers, secondary sources, the *Congressional Record*, and the corpus of presidential remarks and speeches.

Finding Popular Presidential Communications

Many presidency scholars, including Tulis and Kernell, focus on the mode of popular presidential communication. These scholars posit that spoken rhetoric is inherently different from written communication. However, by decoupling two dimensions of popular presidential communication—mode and audience—I am able to show that the focus on speech alone is largely the result of inaccurate historical reflection based on our own contemporary understanding of the presidency. Instead, it is important to understand both how the president communicates and to whom that communication is directed.

To get a fuller picture of the presidency as an institution, I thought it necessary to obtain a more complete set of nineteenth- and early twentieth-century presidential rhetoric. Laracey's (2002) work piqued my interest in what kind of information historical newspapers could provide. Since many of these newspapers have been digitized in the last decade, this seemed like an obvious place to find popular presidential communications of nineteenth-century presidents.

I began this project by collecting instances of spoken popular presidential communication from Washington through Coolidge, since these speeches had not been compiled anywhere. I began by searching digitized historical newspapers using keywords.[8] These searches returned headlines with related articles that included these keywords. For the early presidents, I used the Early American Newspaper collection, the Nineteenth Century Newspaper collection, and the American Periodicals series. I added the *Chicago Tribune* for searches beginning in 1851, the *New York Times* for searches from 1855 onward, the *Washington Post* and *Los Angeles Times* beginning with 1877, and the *San Francisco Chronicle* beginning with 1881. Once all these newspapers were in existence (1881), I stopped searching the other collections.[9] These five newspapers represent a large section of the country and often reprinted stories from other newspapers, providing even more geographic coverage.

The point of these newspaper searches was to create a more complete record of presidential speech, not to provide a complete record of news-paper coverage of presidents. I compared my search results to existing compilations of presidential speeches and to accounts in numerous presidential biographies. This evaluation allowed me to test the completeness of my searches for presidential speeches. Based on that comparison, it is reasonable to conclude that my search underreports the amount of spoken popular presidential communication. It is possible that more examples will be uncovered as more papers are digitized. There were various reasons for this underreporting, including articles that fell outside the search criteria, lack of clarity in articles as to which train stations were visited (especially likely on presidential tours), and the fact that some speeches were published only in newspapers that have not physically survived or have not yet been digitized. For example, Rutherford B. Hayes, Benjamin Harrison, William McKinley, and Theodore Roosevelt made many whistle-stops in one day, and newspapers might list only the towns they visited without recording the words they spoke. Or newspapers might mention that the president offered a speech or a greeting without providing a word-for-word transcription. Occasionally, there was a report of the president visiting a town but no allusion to any speech or other utterance. I did not count these events as speeches—a very conservative strategy. Errors in my recording of speeches would primarily be attributable to speaking events that were not recorded anywhere or that were recorded in sources I did not have access to. In any case, there is no reason to think that such errors would invalidate my conclusion that there is more public presidential speech than scholars often acknowledge.

I coded information about each speech, including the date, the greeting, the newspaper in which it was published, the date it was published, the location where the speech was given, and the topic of the speech. I also coded each speech as having substantive or ceremonial content. In the end, I collected more than three thousand instances of spoken popular presidential communication. While most of these speeches had already been discovered, they had never been compiled and systematically coded. These data provide a more complete picture of presidential rhetoric across the entirety of the institution. I complemented these data I collected with information from the American Presidency Project about presidents from Hoover to Trump.

As Laracey (2002, 2021), Pollard (1947), and others have persuasively argued, the presidential newspaper was critical to an administration's ability to communicate with the public, and this communication took many forms.[10] For purposes of this book, I am interested only in direct communication with the public, rather than the many indirect forms used by early presidents, including anonymous letters, communications with elites that were published in newspapers, and letters written by members of the administration. These communications are all important but beyond the scope of this book.

Organization of the Book

The first two chapters focus on eighteenth- and nineteenth-century presidents. Despite my desire to look at the institution as a whole, the early presidency deserves special attention because it is so often overlooked and misunderstood. My contention is that without an accurate understanding of its early development, the presidency as a whole cannot be put in the proper context. With that in mind, chapter 1 explores the roots of the rhetorical presidency at the Constitutional Convention, in the Constitution, and in the presidencies of George Washington, John Adams, Thomas Jefferson, James Madison, James Monroe, and John Quincy Adams. I find that the Constitution created a vague institution with plenty of opportunity for rhetorical leadership. Washington and Adams saw communication with the public as a vital aspect of their leadership strategies. Jefferson and his immediate successors were more constrained in their public appeals, but when circumstances required it, they too communicated with the people.

Chapter 2 looks closely at the presidency of Andrew Jackson and his strategy of seeking public support in writing, which originated in the early nineteenth century. I investigate John Tyler's rhetorical attempts to establish legitimacy through written rhetoric as the first "accidental" president and James K. Polk's efforts to mirror Jackson's going-public strategy. Polk was less successful than Jackson because his grip on the Democratic Party was incomplete. I also look at Abraham Lincoln's successful use of written communication to lead public opinion through the Civil War. Although Lincoln's approach fits poorly with the others covered in this chapter, it illustrates both the uniqueness of the circumstances and his deep understanding of the media landscape.

In Chapter 3 I examine the first significant increase in the frequency of spoken popular presidential communication, which occurred in the post–Civil War era. This era was marked by the growth of the railroad, the most important but certainly not the only technological innovation that drove change in presidential communication strategies. I look closely at Andrew Johnson's often maligned "swing around the circle" to illustrate how the media environment constrained the persuadable public. I also examine Rutherford B. Hayes and Benjamin Harrison, two often overlooked presidents who actually set important precedents that would develop over the next fifty years. Last, I consider exceptions to the trend of more frequent communication: Chester Arthur and Grover Cleveland. The increased frequency of spoken rhetoric can be linked to technological innovation and political pressure rather than a changed constitutional norm. Moreover, the trend toward more frequent speech is not entirely consistent, suggesting nuanced incentive structures.

Chapter 4 tackles the changing content of spoken popular presidential communication around the turn of the twentieth century. I consider two aspects of content: substantive versus ceremonial content and intellectual content. I do this in a number of ways. First, I use linear regression to look at the intellectual content of annual messages, State of the Union addresses, and inaugural addresses from 1789 to 2017. I also consider Wilson's role in changing the content of spoken popular presidential communication. I find that the significance of Wilson's decision to address a special message to Congress in person is often overstated and that the groundwork for going public was set long before 1913.

Chapter 5 discusses important technological innovations such as radio, television, and Air Force One. Moreover, I examine the golden age
of presidential communication, when presidents could truly reach and
potentially persuade a national audience. I also include an analysis of the
greeting in all annual messages and State of the Union addresses to test
the hypothesis that Congress was the main audience for rhetoric with
policy content before Wilson's presidency. Here, I find that presidents
failed to address their annual messages to popular audiences until the
mid-twentieth century, further undercutting the notion that Wilson was
a singular catalyst for change.

Chapter 6 examines the most recent period of presidential communication. In this chapter I concentrate on the discursive media environment, polarization, and partisanship, which have led presidents to address narrow audiences and focus on motivating their own bases rather
than broader persuasion. I look closely at the audiences for interviews of
Clinton, Obama, and Trump.

The conclusion assesses the evolution of popular presidential communication and the development of the presidency and American politics more broadly.

1

Going Elite: George Washington to
John Q. Adams, 1789–1828

In the nation's earliest days, the persuadable public was small, given that the franchise was limited and electoral incentives were weak. Presidential electors were chosen by state legislators, which also chose senators. This system meant that effectively one thousand men were responsible for electing the president (McDonald 1976). Constrained by limited technology, a newspaper industry economically dependent on direct associations with political parties, and a very limited franchise, the earliest presidents directed most of their rhetoric at elite groups. When George Washington and James Monroe toured the country, they were met by greeting committees made up of mayors and aldermen. Similarly, their written communications were directed almost exclusively at elite audiences, including town meetings and state legislatures. Occasionally these presidents addressed the earliest forms of interest groups, including the Society of Cincinnati and veterans of the American Revolution.[1] Given the low literacy rate and limited franchise, this strategy made sense (Pasley 2001). In fact, these elites *were* the public, as only white property-owning men could participate in politics.

These presidents addressed citizens in the service of building national unity in the fledging country, and although these efforts may seem largely ceremonial by today's standards, there was no more important political task at the time. As limited as their prospects may have been, these earliest presidents still sought and developed a relationship with the American public, cementing the importance of this connection for future leaders.

Despite the size of their audience, the communication strategies of these early presidents remain important for three reasons: First, a relationship between the president and the public has been present since the founding of the nation; thus, the creation of the Constitution and the nation's early presidents are a logical place to begin this investigation. Second, how the founders themselves envisioned the relationship between the president and the people guides our understanding of the evolution of presidential rhetoric. In other words: is presidential communication aimed at the public an essential part of democracy, or is this rhetoric a perversion of the intended system? Third, by tracing the development of presidential rhetoric in the earliest days of the republic, the factors that inspired its metamorphosis can be identified.

This chapter begins by discussing the origins of the presidency in the Constitution to establish the founders' view on presidential rhetoric. I look at the rhetorical strategies of each of the first six presidents to show that even though opportunities for reaching the people were quite limited, presidents embraced these openings when necessary to further their political goals. I also reexamine Thomas Jefferson's decision to send the annual message to Congress in writing rather than appearing in person. This episode is a key development in evolving communication strategies. If a constitutional norm against presidents speaking publicly about policy issues existed, we would expect Jefferson or his supporters to cite this norm as a reason to implement this change. In conclusion, I find that although the audience for these presidents was small, persuasion was difficult, and reaching the public was often fraught, there is little evidence of a pervasive norm against popular rhetoric.

The Constitutional Convention

The framers of the US Constitution were famously suspicious of executive power. In fact, the founders' first effort contained no executive. However, this loose confederation of states quickly proved unworkable, and a second effort was undertaken. Some of the delegates at the Constitutional Convention remained cautious about executive power, while others believed the lack of an executive to provide "energy and direction" was the fatal flaw of the Articles of Confederation (Beeman 2010, 9).[2] George Washington and James Madison were among those who advocated for a president (Beeman 2010, 21). Similarly, Benjamin Franklin's experience abroad had convinced him that the country needed a stronger, more unified central government. Others argued against the creation of an executive and feared a strong central government (McDonald 1994; Laracey 2002; Ketcham 2003; Beeman 2010).

For the founders, "the nature of presidential power was among the most confusing subjects they faced all summer" (Beeman 2010, 230). The delegates had various concepts of an executive based on "their individual temperaments and personal experiences in government" (McDonald 1994, 160). They disagreed on numerous issues, including whether there should be a unitary executive or whether a council would be a better setup to keep the office in check. The founders also disagreed about the appropriate term and electoral mechanism (Ketcham 2003).

David K. Nichols describes two understandings of the presidency and the president's relationship with the public expressed at the convention: Alexander Hamilton's view of a "powerful executive with institutional barriers to popular influence," and James Wilson's notion of "presidential authority as a direct outgrowth of popular support." Related to Wilson's idea, Gouverneur Morris thought that, "because of his unique claim to represent national opinion," the president would serve as a "valuable counterweight to the legislature" (Nichols 1994, 36, 44). All these views existed simultaneously that summer in Philadelphia.

Evidence from the Constitutional Convention suggests ambiguity and uncertainty surrounded the exact nature of the presidency (Beeman 2010; Ketcham 2003; McDonald 1994). In addition, as with almost every aspect of the new government, it is likely delegates had divergent and sometimes even competing views about executive power (Nichols 1994; McDonald 1994). The most likely scenario is one in which some of the founders envisioned a strong presidency with a direct connection to the people, while others did not. This unresolved tension has clear implications for how we should think about popular presidential communication. The presidency as an institution was open to interpretation, whether the president chose to cultivate a relationship with the public or chose a more constrained path. As the following discussion shows, in practice, presidents quickly realized that their relationship with the public was essential to the unity of the nation and an important source of political power. However, both practical and political considerations influenced how this relationship between the executive and the people would develop.

Defining the Presidency in the Constitution

In establishing the executive branch, Article II of the Constitution is vague and brief, suggesting little consensus among the founders. While the duties of Congress were well defined, the role of the president was much more amorphous, lending support to the argument that the framers were unsure how the nation's new executive branch would function (McDonald 1994, 3). A closer look at Article II indicates that the founders had no unifying vision about the relationship between the president and the public. Instead, "the original understanding of the presidency confirms what is apparent from a reading of the text of Article II, namely that the Constitution authorizes either an active or a passive presidency" (McDonald 1994, 185). The Constitution vests executive power in the presidency in Article II, section 1. Much of the symbolic power of the presidency comes from his position as commander in chief, set out in

Article II, section 2. Section 2 also gives the president the pardon power, the ability to appoint ambassadors and judges, and the power to make treaties. Section 3 establishes the "state of the Union" and, perhaps most importantly, the power to ensure that the laws are faithfully executed. This open-ended clause has allowed tremendous growth in executive power (Genovese 2006, 9). In sum, the Constitution established a general and vague outline for executive power. As this chapter shows, the earliest presidents immediately started to fill in the contours of this new institution, including establishing a relationship with the people.

The Founding Presidents and Their Audience

Another way to determine the role the founders envisioned for the president is to analyze how the first six presidents—George Washington, John Adams, Thomas Jefferson, James Madison, James Monroe, and John Quincy Adams[3]—behaved in office, as these men were in the unique position of serving in the government they had created. A close examination of these presidencies shows multiple and evolving conceptions of the appropriate role of the executive in government and of the relationship between the president and the people. Views ranged from a constrained presidency to one dependent on a connection with the public. However, as the historical record shows, even those presidents who had a cautious view of the role of popular presidential communication adopted a more ambitious view when the political incentives were strong enough. In all cases, these political incentives were mediated by technological constraints in this early period; loosely defined, elite-centered political parties; a franchise limited to property-owning white men; and a media environment defined by partisanship and administration-sponsored newspapers.

Presidents in this early period were significantly hampered by a limited ability to travel. Many roads were dangerous and poorly maintained. For Washington, a good day on the road meant covering about thirty

miles (Ellis 2008). In addition, printing and distribution capabilities were
much more primitive than they would be later in the nineteenth century.
Moreover, the first six presidents had an interest in appearing "above
party," or nonpartisan, and they had relatively weak electoral ties (Ketcham 2003). Although these first presidents considered themselves duty-
bound to the citizens of the United States, there was a much narrower
conception of citizenship in the early nineteenth century. Their notion
of an "enlightened electorate" was a group of citizens who were highly
informed, educated, and engaged. In the late eighteenth and early nineteenth centuries this meant being a white property-owning male who was
literate—a relatively small portion of the population. The makeup of the
president's audience was and continues to be an important part of how
presidents view and leverage their relationship with the people. In this
early period, a limited public coupled with significant technological constraints made the incentives for reaching out to the people quite modest.
However, there were circumstances under which these early presidents
communicated directly with the public.

In an effort to determine the immediate audience a president was
addressing, and thus who he was actually trying to persuade, I used the
salutation and other information provided in the reporting surrounding his speech. Greetings ranged from specific group names to general
openings such as "Fellow Citizens." Even in this early period, presidential speeches often reached the whole nation, even though it might have
taken weeks. Initially, Washington and Monroe addressed greeting committees composed of elite members of whatever city or town they were
visiting. These men met the president on the edge of town or in the town
center, presented the president with a formal greeting, and received the
president's reply. Andrew Jackson and Martin Van Buren were also met
by greeting committees but occasionally addressed the citizenry more
generally. By the time John Tyler toured in 1849, the majority of his rhetoric (77 percent) was directed to local audiences. This trend continued
until Woodrow Wilson and Calvin Coolidge used regular press conferences to address newspaper correspondents.

Imagining a Nation: The Presidency of George Washington
(1789–1797)

At least part of the founders' willingness to create this potentially power-ful but vague executive office was their comfort with George Washington, who everyone at the convention knew would be the nation's first presi-dent (Waldstreicher 1997; Beeman 2010; Genovese 2006). Upon taking office, Washington quickly found that his position was an inherently rhe-torical one.

For the American people, the act of becoming a nation involved more than winning a victory over the British. In fact, although the Revolution-ary War established the basis for national sovereignty and political com-munity, "it left unresolved the question of who that political community included, and the symbolic representation of the nation remained com-paratively weak, very localized, and quite thin" (Spillman 1997, 23). The failure of the Articles of Confederation raised the stakes for the young country.

Even after ratification of the Constitution, questions remained. The framers of the Constitution had not reached a consensus on many issues, and the Anti-Federalists were skeptical of the newly established federal government with the president at its head. In fact, tension about whether "liberty was to be associated with the states or with national sovereignty" remained until after the Civil War (Spillman 1997, 23). In sum, the contin-ued existence of the new nation was in no way assured.

Despite his popularity, Washington's biggest challenge as the nation's first president was creating a national identity for the American people. In an effort to establish this imagined community in the United States, Washington addressed the people through speeches with relative fre-quency. Though not constitutionally mandated, he began his presidency with an inaugural address that laid out his vision for the new country, and such a speech quickly became the norm (Zarefsky 2002, 24). Wash-ington's inaugural address was drafted by James Madison, widely re-garded as the "father of the Constitution." Given the circumstances, it is

"inconceivable that Washington would have presented such an address
... if either he or Madison had believed the Constitution was intended to
establish even an implicit norm prohibiting the president from making
speeches on matters of national policy" (Lucas 2008, 40). Washington
also established the practice of appearing before Congress to give his
annual message. However, the majority of Washington's spoken rhetoric
came while on tour. During his eight years in office, Washington embarked on three tours and gave at least thirty-six speeches to the public
while traveling (Ellis 2008; Pluta 2014).

Washington faced a number of obstacles in his desire to reach the
public. Time-consuming and sometimes dangerous travel conditions, as
well as limited printing and distribution capabilities, significantly constrained the new president. Washington was nearly universally loved and
admired, but he was also quiet and aloof. His ill-fitting dentures made
public speaking difficult and potentially embarrassing (Chernow 2010).
The time and effort required to speak to the people indicate how important Washington was not just as the executive officer but also as the
symbol of a fledgling nation whose very existence was tenuous. The quest
for national unity was pressing enough to warrant Washington's efforts.

Washington went on tour because of his desire, as he stated in 1791,
"to win the goodwill, the support of the people for the General Government" and to "discern the true trend of public opinion" (Henderson 1923,
4). On his tour of New England (October 15–November 13, 1789), where
Anti-Federalist sentiment was strong, Washington hoped to demonstrate
"the energy, dignity and potential power of the presidency" (Ferling
2009, 54). Similarly, in the South, where opposition to the Constitution
continued after adjournment of the First Congress, Washington went on
tour (March 21–June 12, 1791) in the hopes of strengthening the principles
of national unity and centralized federal government (Henderson 1923).

These reasons may seem ceremonial by today's standards, but in 1791
there was no greater political challenge (Ellis 2004). Archibald Henderson aptly characterizes Washington's travels as "American Democracy on
Grand tour," and his speeches were intended to "evoke their [the people's]

Table 1.1: George Washington's Tours (1789–1797)

Dates	States Visited	Number of Days	Number of Speeches	Themes
October 15–November 13, 1789	CT, MA, NH[a]	29	13	National unity and federal government
August 14–22, 1790	RI	8	2	National unity and federal government
March 21–June 12, 1791[b]	MD, VA, SC, NC, GA	83	21	National unity and federal government

[a]Washington did not stop in New Jersey and Delaware because he had just visited there on his preinaugural tour. He did not visit New York and Pennsylvania because they were temporary capitals and "citizens already enjoyed access to the national government" (Moats 2010, 50).

[b]The tour ended on June 3 in North Carolina. The rest of the trip was spent returning to Mount Vernon (Henderson 1923).

support of the general government through attachment to his own person" (1923, xx). In this sense, the American presidency was personal from the very beginning. Table 1.1 lists the details of Washington's tours.

An often overlooked aspect of Washington's presidency was that he traveled with a speechwriter: Major William Jackson. Because Washington "was wholly lacking in the readiness and volubility of an orator," whenever he received a query from a group on tour, it was his custom to present a formal written reply at a later time; Washington would draft the broad outlines of the reply, and Major Jackson would finalize it (Henderson 1923, 15). Importantly, no constitutional impediment was cited as the reason for the written reply. Instead, Washington's abilities, or lack thereof, necessitated a written rather than a spoken response.

On tour and in other rhetoric, Washington linked the glory of the Revolution to the federal government in an attempt to build a national identity (Waldstreicher 1997, 117; Chernow 2010). The founders were resistant to the development of factions because they feared these groups could cleave the tenuously bonded country. In a letter "To the Hebrew Congregations in the Cities of Philadelphia, New York, Charleston, and Richmond" dated January 4, 1791, Washington wrote, "The power & goodness of the Almighty were strongly manifested in the events of our glorious revolution; and his kind interposition in our behalf, has been no less visible in the establishment of our present equal government." In this letter, the president linked the Revolution to the current government of the United States. He expressed a similar sentiment in a May 16, 1789, letter "To the Mayor, Eldermen, and City Council of Philadelphia": "When I contemplate the interposition of Providence, as it was visibly manifested, in guiding us through the revolution, in preparing us for the reception of a general government, and in conciliating the good will of the people of America towards one another after its adoption; I feel myself oppressed and almost overwhelmed with a sense of the Divine Munificence" (*Providence Gazette*, June 6, 17891). Many of Washington's speeches on tour linked the "glory of the War of Independence with the latent glory of the newly established U.S." (Ellis 2004, 196).

The rise of partisanship created a new incentive for Washington to communicate with the public in his second term (1793–1797). During this time, Washington tried not only to gauge but also to lead public opinion on foreign policy during the debate surrounding the Jay Treaty. Signed in April 1796, the treaty with Great Britain was wildly unpopular, and the Federalists set out to conflate support for a popular president with support for the treaty.[4] In this effort, Washington inserted himself "boldly and forthrightly at several junctures in the public debate, each time strongly helping the pro-treaty side" (Estes 2001, 127). Newspapers widely reprinted Washington's letters supporting the treaty. The president's "skillful deployment of particular political skills . . . turned the tide of public opinion" and helped bring about approval of the Jay Treaty in the House of Representatives (Estes 2001, 128). The Federalists encouraged citizens to send petitions to Congress, and the main instrument in that campaign was George Washington (Estes 2001, 156).

Despite being frustrated by the press in his second term, Washington personally arranged for the publication of his Farewell Address in the *Pennsylvania Packet and Daily Advertiser* and signed his name to the document, not attempting to hide its authorship (Pollard 1947). Addressed to "Friends and Fellow Citizens," it was eventually published by "nearly every newspaper in the nation," and in it, Washington laid out a vision for the country's future (Furstenberg 2006, 7). In his final rhetorical act, Washington used his connection with the public, as narrow as it was, to "advance the interests of the Federalist Party, and he hoped, ensure its domination for years to come" (Ferling 2009, 470). Though often considered a foreign policy treatise, the document was in fact a "nationalist text," spelling out potential threats to the young nation, including geographic disunion, factions, and interference from foreign powers (Furstenberg 2006, 8).

Washington's Farewell Address illustrates an important point: despite the emphasis on spoken rhetoric as an essential aspect of the "modern" presidency, early presidents' written communications cannot easily be dismissed. Given the constraints associated with both travel and the dissemination of information, written rhetoric was the only efficient way to reach any meaningful portion of the public—keeping in mind that literacy rates remained low in the United States at this time. Moreover, many of the earliest presidents, including Washington and Jefferson, were much more skilled as writers than orators. Simply put, giving speeches did not play to their strengths. Washington's longest tours lasted twenty-nine and eighty-four days, and he still reached only a small portion of the country. Therefore, it is not surprising that the president would use written communication to address the public as a whole. Of course, the "public" was quite narrow at this point, but this would change drastically over time and have significant implications for presidential rhetoric, as I show later in this book. Until the maturation of the railroad and development of the telegraph and radio in the late nineteenth and early twentieth centuries, the use of written communication was both logical and politically expedient.

As the president of the Constitutional Convention and the first president of the country, Washington's rhetorical behavior and outlook on presidential leadership should be instructive to an understanding of the constitutionally appropriate role of the American president. Given his stature and genuine concern for the nation's well-being, it is unlikely that Washington would do anything to blatantly contradict his understanding of the Constitution or the founders' intent (Lucas 2008). Washington knew he was setting important precedents, given the ambiguity of the newly created executive office, and he seemed to understand intuitively "that the presidency, if properly established, would be dual in nature, chief executive officer but also ritualistic and ceremonial head of state" (McDonald 1994, 216; Chernow 2010).

Washington's influence continued after he left office, as a mythology was built around the former general and president. In addition to myths about the man himself, Washington's successors relied on mythology surrounding the Revolution, the Declaration of Independence, and the Constitution, as well as the mythology of Americans as a chosen people, in an effort to continue to build national unity (Spillman 1997, 24). The use of this kind of imagery was purposeful because political mythology is one way to build imagined communities. Myths are culturally meaningful stories that provide human beings with an understanding of their place in the universe (Dorsey 2002, 136). They are effective because they "are able to reach both into the past and the future, allowing us to change with the times without completely redefining the nation" (Stuckcy 2018, 97).

John Adams (1797), Thomas Jefferson (1801), and John Quincy Adams (1825) referred to the Revolutionary War in their inaugural addresses. James Madison (1812), James Monroe (1818, 1820, 1821, 1824), and John Quincy Adams (1827) addressed the Revolution in one or more of their annual messages.

In the Shadow of Washington: The Rhetorical Presidency
of John Adams (1797–1801)

After eight years, Washington set a final important precedent by refusing
to run for a third term. His successor, John Adams, was in a difficult position because he faced many of the same barriers to a relationship with
the public that Washington had, without the former general's charisma
or stature. Moreover, Adams had the misfortune of following one of the
most beloved and revered figures in American political history at a time
when partisanship was taking hold in the nascent country. Adams faced
stiff resistance from Jefferson, his vice president, who was from the opposition party, the Democrat-Republicans. This left Adams isolated and
seemingly with no one but his wife, Abigail, to support him (Ellis 2001).
Though he lacked Washington's universal appeal, Adams followed many
of the precedents set by Washington, delivering all his annual messages
to Congress and replies to the House and Senate in person (Lucas 2008).[5]
In many ways, Adams saw his administration as a continuation of Washington's, so he continued these traditions.

Evidence that Adams admired Washington and was likely following
his precedents can be found in his inaugural address. Adams profusely
praised Washington, describing him as a "citizen . . . regulated by pru-
dence, justice, temperance, and fortitude" who merited "the gratitude of
his fellow-citizens, commanded the highest praises of foreign nations,
and secured immortal glory with posterity." The new president continued: "This example has been recommended to the imitation of his successors by both Houses of Congress and by the voice of the legislatures
and the people throughout the nation."

Like Washington, Adams was concerned with leading public opinion, especially on issues related to foreign policy. Adams called the first
special session of Congress and appeared before the legislature to deliver
a special message on May 16, 1797. In this message, Adams discussed the
ongoing hostilities with France and the need to strengthen naval defenses.
I found no debate in the *Annals of Congress* surrounding Adams's appear-

ance, suggesting there was little sentiment that the president should avoid addressing the legislature in person.

The XYZ affair provided Adams an opportunity to solidify the relationship between the president and the people.[6] Whereas Washington and the Federalists had harnessed public opinion in the debate surrounding the Jay Treaty, Adams took the same approach with the XYZ affair. Citizens from all parts of the country sent petitions and declarations to the president in support of his position against the French. In total, almost three hundred petitions arrived in Philadelphia between April 1798 and the end of March 1799 (Ray 1983). As was the custom, the original letters and Adams's responses were reprinted in newspapers across the nation (Waldstreicher 1997). Additionally, 106 of the letters, along with Adams's replies, were compiled in a volume published in 1798 and titled *A Selection of the Patriotic Addresses, to the President of the United States.* This book included missives from across the country and from groups representing inhabitants of various towns, state legislatures, college students, and grand juries. The letter writers expressed support for the administration and its policies toward France.

In his replies, Adams reiterated the support he was receiving for his policy positions. As an example, in response to the Massachusetts legislature, Adams wrote, "The solemn pledge of your selves to support every measure which the government of the United States, at this momentous period, may see fit to adopt to protect the commerce and preserve the independence of our country must afford an important encourage to the national government, and contribute greatly to the union of people throughout all the States" (Adams and Austin 1798, 32). This kind of response, which thanked the letter writer and also expressed support for the federal government, was typical of the letters Adams wrote. The publication of these documents shows how important they were to the politics of the time.

These lively exchanges between the president and the public helped bring legitimacy to the still fragile federal government. Citizens gathered both to write the initial petitions and to receive Adams's replies. Waldstreicher describes the "weeks-long drama of the meetings, addresses, responses, and their reception, punctuated at every step by publication," as "an incredibly potent example of acting locally while thinking nationally" (1997, 162). These meetings allowed participation to expand beyond white, literate, property-owning men. Women and the illiterate were able to attend these meetings and hear the president's responses (Waldstreicher 1997). Meetings like these were one of the few opportunities for broad political participation in the early republic.

This interaction between the president and the public generated favorable news coverage and positive shifts in public opinion toward the president's position (Young 2014). In summary, "like Washington before him, Adams engaged the American people in a dialogue. It was a conversation that helped to solidify the idea in the public imagination that the American president was a popular leader and that they, the people, had a relationship with him" (Young 2014, 122). In this attempt to lead public opinion, Adams demonstrated the power of the already evolving relationship between the president and the people.

Washington and Adams shared a concern that the public be well informed about political affairs. Adams saw that presenting information to Congress was one way to keep the public abreast of current affairs, as messages to Congress would be reprinted in the newspaper, where people could access them. As Adams wrote to his secretary of state in November 1799, laying out information in a message to Congress regarding France would allow the public "to judge from correct and authentic documents" (Pollard 1947, 44). Adams's thinking here points to an important notion that would endure for his successors: though messages might be directed to Congress, they would be dissected by the press and followed closely by the public.[7] Presidents were well aware that their correspondence with Congress was subject to public scrutiny, and rather than view the public as a secondary audience, presidents often treated the people as equal to the legislature. The audiences Washington and Adams addressed were minuscule compared with those presidents would have even three decades later. Despite this, Washington and Adams set important precedents for the annual message and its audience.

Despite facing significant barriers to direct access, both Washington and Adams saw even limited communication with the public as an essential element of the presidency. Encouraged by the desire to boost acceptance of the newly formed federal government and to shape public opinion on foreign policy, Washington and Adams reached out to the American people through both writing and speech.

The First Transfer of Power: Thomas Jefferson
(1801–1809)

Thomas Jefferson was the first president to preside over a transfer of power from one party to another, and he faced unique political incentives for popular presidential communication. The new president needed to claim legitimacy and assure citizens that the change in leadership would not disrupt the democratic experiment. After spending twelve years complaining about the Federalists' pomp and circumstance, Jefferson was eager to provide an alternative understanding of presidential power and leadership. For many of Jefferson's supporters, the election of 1800 signified a second American Revolution that led to its own political subculture, and they "repeatedly dramatized their victory as a new birth of liberty" (Waldstreicher 1997, 187; Pasley 2013).

The new president's first opportunity to distinguish himself from his predecessors was his inaugural address. Jefferson understood "that style is substance, and he delighted supporters all over the country with his studied refusal of ostentation" (Waldstreicher 1997, 190). The president-elect began by walking to his inauguration rather than taking a horse and carriage (Ellis 2008). On the way, Jefferson told a crowd that he "generally disliked formal addresses" (Waldstreicher 1997, 187). Jefferson never went on tour, he sent the annual message to Congress in writing, and he consciously tried to avoid any quasi-monarchical behavior. As president, Jefferson worked hard to "republicanize" the presidency (McDonald 1994), at least in part because this was what his partisan supporters wanted.

Washington and Adams had used the newspaper to communicate the administration's goals to the public, but Jefferson took this strategy to new heights. The *National Intelligencer*, which was often called the "government organ," and its editor Samuel Harrison Smith provided Jefferson with a powerful tool to reach his supporters directly (Laracey 2002, 59). The existence of an administration newspaper significantly decreased the need for the president to address the public, as the paper articulated his political positions to supporters (Pasley 2001; Laracey 2002). The newspaper not only carried Jefferson's speeches but also included all the "federal government's office notices, proclamations, and advertisements" (Laracey 2002, 60). However, the *National Intelligencer* likely constrained Jefferson's ability to reach those who disagreed with him. The president's opponents probably would not spend a significant amount of time reading the administration's newspaper. Instead, the opposition would likely be engaging with Federalist newspapers that were opposed to the administration and its policies. Jefferson cultivated a deep relationship with Smith and used the newspaper to keep the public informed on matters of government. Additionally, the newspaper reprinted letters Jefferson received from groups, along with his replies (Laracey 2002). This reinforced the relationship with the public that Washington and Adams had built and relied on.

Although Jefferson spoke to the public less frequently than Washington, his inaugural addresses, particularly his first one, proved much more important than those of either of his predecessors. Jefferson's inauguration was a much simpler ceremony, but his speech contained a lot more substance and therefore had a more significant impact (Cunningham 2001). Having presided over the first transfer of power in the young nation, Jefferson stated his political principles and called for unity after a bruising election battle and newly solidified partisanship. As would become the custom, Jefferson gave Smith an advance copy of the inaugural address to print in the newspaper so the audience could follow along (Laracey 2002; Meacham 2012, 92). The speech was subsequently reprinted in newspapers throughout the country and in Europe (Cunningham 2001; Laracey 2002). The fact that Jefferson's speech was initially spoken was of little consequence to the tens of thousands of people who would eventually read the message.

Jefferson expanded the power of the presidency in many ways, despite his stated aversion to executive power. Though he publicly complained about the behavior of Washington and Adams, he too strove to develop a relationship with the public. Jefferson understood his political strengths and weaknesses and kept them in mind as he cultivated a link to the people. Perhaps most important, like many men of this age, Jefferson was a weak speaker but a brilliant writer (McDonald 1976, 39; Meacham 2012, 348), so it was to his political (and practical) advantage to conduct most of his communications in writing.

Jefferson's decision to deliver his annual message to Congress in writing is often treated as his most consequential rhetorical choice. This decision is used as an example of the founders' view of constitutionally appropriate presidential behavior. However, as this chapter has illustrated, there was little consensus about what constituted appropriate presidential communication. Moreover, Jefferson had a number of important logistical and political incentives that led him to institute this change in practice, but strictly speaking, none of them appeared to be constitutional.

By 1801, partisan lines had clearly been drawn. So rather than having a constitutional reason for addressing Congress in writing, Jefferson had strategic reasons for avoiding a speech before the legislature. The *National Intelligencer* printed Jefferson's brief message explaining why he was changing the custom and then reprinted the address in its entirety on December 9, 1801. No editorial commentary was included. Jefferson explained that he was sending the message in writing for the "convenience of the legislature, to the economy of their time, to their relief from embarrassment of immediate answers on subjects not yet before them and to the benefits hence resulting in the public affairs," and he trusted "that a procedure found in these motives will meet their approbation." Jefferson failed to mention the Constitution and did not assume this change would be acceptable. Similarly, the *Annals of Congress* included Jefferson's letter and message but recorded no commentary from members of Congress.

The *Citizen* (December 12, 1801) criticized Jefferson's decision:

> It is thought that the illustrious Chief intends to lay before the two Houses the state of the Republic by message. This will be a dreadful innovation—a sad disorganizing measure. It will, however, form a new, important, and brilliant era in executive forms. Nor will it be unattended, with beneficial affects [*sic*]. By Message, the president can, and no doubt will, communicate to the two Houses the state of the Nation as fully as by speech the form adopted by his predecessors. But a message will require no answer. Consequently the time of the legislature and the money of the country will not be spent in useless and irrating [*sic*] debate.

This editorial seemed to suggest that while the change to a written message was less than ideal, the elimination of a congressional reply was a positive development. Again, there was no mention of the appropriateness of a written message as opposed to a spoken one.

The elimination of a reply from Congress was a practical change. Because members of Congress were required to appear before the president to deliver it, this posed two problems: parking for carriages in front of the new White House was limited, and a congressional reply implied unity, which no longer existed. As partisan conflict grew in Congress, a unified response to some of the controversial questions covered in the president's message would have been elusive (Meacham 2012, 92). The debate surrounding responses to Adams's messages illustrated as much. Moreover, letters between Jefferson and Benjamin Rush allude to avoiding "bloody conflicts" with the Federalists as one reason to abandon speaking in front of Congress (Laracey 2021).

Jefferson also faced political pressure from Representative Matt Lyon, who had played a critical role in the election of 1800.[8] Lyon's one vote from Vermont gave Jefferson the nine states he needed to defeat Aaron Burr. A year earlier, Lyon had won fame when he was jailed under the Alien and Sedition Acts, and upon his release, he was treated like a conquering hero by the Anti-Federalists. His distaste for presidents appearing before Congress in person was well known (Pasley 2001).

Jefferson decided to abandon the reading of his message to Congress because of the rise of partisanship, a desire to usher in his political ideology, and his poor speaking ability. As Forrest McDonald adeptly summarized, "In point of practice, the change reflects Jefferson's realization that he was simply no good at dealing with men in the aggregate" (1994, 39). If, in fact, a constitutional norm had existed, it seems likely that Jefferson would have cited that norm as a reason for the change.

Jefferson's precedent lasted 112 years until Woodrow Wilson changed the practice in 1913. Jefferson had "reconstructed the terms and conditions of national government," including delivering the annual message to Congress in writing (Skowronek 1997, 63). At the same time, as the nation grew the annual message got longer, covered many topics, and was written like a report, making the reversion to a spoken message increasingly impractical. Despite their length, congressional clerks read the annual messages, and they were published in newspapers throughout the country. Newspapers widely discussed the messages and treated them as presidential pronouncements on matters of policy. In sum, there were few incentives for presidents to change the mode of the annual message for the next century. Wilson's reasons for reviving the practice of delivering the message in person are discussed at length in chapter 4.

Following in Jefferson's Footsteps:
James Madison (1809–1817) and James Monroe (1817–1825)

Jefferson's successors, James Madison and James Monroe, had fewer reasons to prove their republican credentials and communicate with the public. They both enjoyed the advantage of having administration newspapers, and for a short time, at least, partisanship seemed to be waning. The precedents Jefferson set were mostly upheld by his fellow Democratic-Republicans. Madison's adherence to Jeffersonian principles should not be surprising, given that "no one on earth was closer to him [Jefferson] politically" than Madison (Meacham 2012, 439; Rutland 1990).

Madison had another important similarity to Jefferson: difficulty connecting with people through speech. As Robert Allen Rutland writes, "In Madison the voters knew what they were getting: a short, baldish, honest man whose speeches were hard to hear—but on paper those speeches made a lot of sense" (1990, 2). Madison also shared Jefferson's view that participation of the most educated and well-informed citizens was vital to the functioning of democracy. This view naturally informed these presidents' communication strategies (Rutland 1990). In fact, they optimized their strategy in terms of audience and used the mode of communication with which they felt most comfortable.

Madison differed from Jefferson in a few politically significant ways. Although the third president never issued a veto, Madison did. More meaningfully, Madison commented in public on these vetoes. Madison vetoed a congressional bill that he thought ran afoul of the First Amendment, and in a reply to Baptist churches he expressed his delight that they supported his position. These letters and replies appeared in newspapers where the public was sure to read them (Rutland 1990). Much like Washington and Adams, Madison was concerned with public opinion in a way that can be understood as "modern." He believed that true republics were "ruled by an interplay between government and society" and that public opinion was a loop that "sustained leaders even as they were shaped by it" (Brookhiser 2011, 105).

James Monroe provided a notable exception to the precedents Jefferson set. Monroe followed in Washington's footsteps and set out on two tours of the country in 1817 and 1819, and newspapers followed his progress (Waldstreicher 1997). On tour, Monroe tackled some of the most important public questions of the day, including the military and the federal government's support of internal improvements (table 1.2).

In the aftermath of the War of 1812, Americans were quick to embrace nonpartisanship in the face of "sectional and partisan developments [that] led some to question whether the American union would

Table 1.2: James Monroe's Tours (1817–1825)

Dates	States Visited	Number of Days	Number of Speeches	Themes
May 31–September 17, 1817	MD, DE, PA, NJ, NY, CT, MA, RI, NH, ME[a], MI[a], VT, OH	109	55	National unity, republican institutions, public education, religious freedom
May 28–June 17, 1818[b]	MD, VA, NC	21	3	Improvements, national unity
March 30–August 8, 1819	VA, NC, SC, GA, TN, KY, IN	100	22	Improvements, national unity, importance of federal government

[a]Territories at the time of the president's visit.

[b]This southern tour was cut short when Monroe was forced to deal with "controversy surrounding General Andrew Jackson's conduct during the recent Seminole War" (Moats 2010, 140).

endure," and Monroe hoped to encourage these feelings while on tour (Waldstreicher 1997, 298). Samuel Putnam Waldo published an account of Monroe's tour in 1819. The book opens with a biographical sketch of Monroe, the circumstances of his election, and his inaugural address, and it closes with his first annual message. The introduction to the section on the tour illustrates the relevance of the relationship between the president and the people. The speeches presented to Monroe and his replies would be described as ceremonial by today's standards, but much like Washington, Monroe referenced the glory of the Revolution and the more recent war to encourage feelings of unity in the still young and loosely bonded nation (Waldo 1819). For example, while in Baltimore, Monroe toured Fort McHenry and assured citizens that "Congress has appropriated large sums of money for the fortification of our coast, and inland frontier, and for the establishment of naval dock yards, and building a navy" (quoted in Waldo 1819, 68). In New York, Monroe pointed out that the "present prosperous condition of our country, is as you justly observe, the best proof of the excellence of our institutions, and of the wisdom with which they have been administered" (quoted in Waldo 1819, 87).

Another common element was that on their tours, Washington and Monroe were often met by greeting committees and received by groups such as the Society of Cincinnati. The groups that interacted with the presidents on these trips provide valuable insight into the growth of American democracy. These early tours by Washington and Monroe were directed at local elites: educated white men who held positions of power in their communities. Similarly, the letters to which presidents replied were from these types of groups. As the franchise in the United States expanded, so did the audiences that presidents tried to reach.

John Quincy Adams (1825–1829)

John Q. Adams was in a difficult position, having lost the popular vote but winning the election in the House of Representatives. This immediately made him vulnerable to charges that he had not been democratically elected. Future presidents in this position, including Rutherford B. Hayes and Benjamin Harrison, would work to establish their legitimacy through popular communication, but Adams avoided this approach. Moreover, throughout his presidency, Jacksonian forces were coalescing and preparing to defeat him in 1828. In summary, there were political incentives for Adams to communicate directly with the people, but he did so quite infrequently because of his "elitist disdain for communicating with the public" (Laracey 2002, 66).

Conclusion

My theoretical approach provides two important observations from this chapter about the early development of popular presidential communication. The first is that when Adams decided to appear before Congress to discuss policy and when Jefferson chose to change the mode of delivery of the annual message, neither they nor their contemporaries cited a constitutional norm. The second is that, even after Jefferson began sending a written annual message to Congress, it remained an important policy document issued by the president and distributed across the country. Neither the press nor the public treated it differently because it was written rather than spoken.

The constitutional origins of the presidency reveal that the founders gave it vague outlines but intended it to be a potentially powerful and popular position. A look at the early presidencies suggests that rather than an agreed-on constitutionally appropriate behavior, Washington and Jefferson exemplified partisan interpretations of the role of the executive. Based on his experience in the military, Washington appreciated that leadership involves more than discharging the constitutional duties of the office. In fact, Washington understood that effective stewardship of the new nation would require him (and his successors) to persuade "Congress, the people, foreign nations, the press and even the remainder of the executive branch" (Lucas 2008, 44). His successor, Adams, followed Washington's example in many ways. The first two presidents made efforts to shape public opinion on issues related to foreign policy.

Jefferson presented a more constrained view of public interaction because of political incentives to do so and because he had an administration newspaper that allowed him to present his views to the public on a regular basis. Jefferson's successors were quick to embrace increased power and a more direct interaction with the public, regardless of partisan positions and an increasingly competitive political environment. The institutionalization of the administration newspaper gave Jefferson and his successors a way to reach their supporters directly.

Political incentives, particularly the desire to provide a symbol of national unity and lead public opinion, shaped the rhetorical choices of the early presidents. These incentives were mediated by limited means of communication and travel, which made it difficult to reach the public through speeches. The lack of popularly based political parties in the early part of the eighteenth century constrained the president's rhetorical choices. Because parties lacked a connection to the public, early presidents had fewer reasons to communicate with the people. These early presidents demonstrated another important factor: the president's own political skill. Politicians in this era were more likely to be skilled writers as opposed to orators. Speech making made little sense if it was not a natural skill. Moreover, the persuadable public was small—not just because the franchise was so restricted but also because the structure of the newspaper system made it very difficult to reach beyond supporters. In sum, these early presidents had limited incentives to even try to persuade the public, yet there are numerous examples of them actively engaging with the people—some of the first illustrations of a practice that would only grow as incentives dictated.

Going Partisan: Andrew Jackson to Abraham Lincoln, 1829–1865

The persuadable public was transformed in the 1820s by the expanded franchise and the emergence of popularly based political parties. In the election of 1828, more than one million votes were cast for president, as virtually all white men were eligible to vote (Cole 2009). Andrew Jackson quickly realized that his connection with the public would be crucial to the success of his administration. This expanded electorate, along with organized mass-based parties and a well-developed administration newspaper, opened up new opportunities for presidents to leverage their relationship with the people.

The newspaper industry grew significantly during this time (Schudson 2001). However, the vast majority of antebellum newspapers were partisan, and editors were "political activists and party organizers filling their newspapers with partisan advocacy" (Baldasty and Rutenbeck 1988, 61). The intersection of mass-based parties and partisan newspapers allowed presidents to easily and effectively reach their own party but gave them little ability to direct their messages to others. Therefore, it made sense for presidents to focus their efforts on motivating their partisans to advance administration goals. Given these circumstances, I call this era "going partisan." This categorization does not mean that antebellum presidents never tried to reach the nation as a whole, but this type of outreach would have required significant effort on their part with potentially little reward.

This chapter explores how written communications served the same purpose as spoken rhetoric later in history (after the advent of radio). This argument is important because it takes on the notion that it was considered constitutionally inappropriate for presidents to discuss policy with the public in the nineteenth century. My account suggests that rather than being limited by constitutional norms, early nineteenth-century presidents were limited by technology and used the administration newspaper to achieve many of the same ends that later presidents accomplished through speech making. This discussion is directly relevant to establishing the roots of going public—that is, presidents taking their case to the public and circumventing the bargaining process in Washington—and illustrating how presidents took advantage of opportunities to do so despite technological limitations.

As noted in the last chapter, touring was the only way early presidents could reach the public directly, unmediated by the press, and for the first half of the 1800s, touring was time-consuming and dangerous. Presidents had no practical way to reach any meaningful portion of the public through speech, so written communication was by far the most reasonable choice.

In examining the dawn of going public, I look closely at the presidencies of Andrew Jackson, John Tyler, and James Polk. Jackson was the first American executive with a real electoral connection to the broader public. Tyler faced difficulties in establishing his legitimacy as the first "accidental" president, but his communication strategies made an important contribution to the broader expansion of popular presidential rhetoric. Polk, a Jackson protégé, tried to use many of the same strategies but faced different constraints. Polk's use of the newspaper to press his case was not unique, but my interpretation places this partisan approach in a larger context. I briefly discuss the next four presidents before concluding with Abraham Lincoln, who is often regarded as the most successful leader of public opinion in the nineteenth century. Lincoln does not fit neatly into

any of my categories, but I include him here because of his significance
to the evolution of the presidency as a whole and because his approach
illustrates the importance of the media environment to presidents' opportunities to communicate with the public.

Using these cases, I argue that scholars have made too much of the
distinction between written and spoken popular presidential communications. Many of the written rhetorical activities undertaken by nineteenth-century presidents had similar objectives as later spoken rhetoric.
By the late nineteenth century, speech was the preferred mode of communication for presidents, with some notable exceptions. This turn to
speech was a natural one, given the demise of the presidential newspaper
and ongoing technological innovations. I also show that the nature of
the media environment constrained who was persuadable in a way that
limited the potential gains of a sustained strategy of going public. Most
of this information is not new, but my analysis provides fresh insight into
how communication strategies developed throughout the nineteenth
century and how they are strikingly similar to twenty-first-century approaches.

The Dawn of Going Public: Andrew Jackson
(1829–1837)

Going public is considered the cornerstone of the modern presidency
(Tulis 1987; Kernell [1986] 1997). The idea of going public is centered on
the president going over the heads of Congress and appealing directly
to the American people. Technology is often considered an important
element of this strategy, but Andrew Jackson was able to go public using
only the administration newspaper. Jackson's presidency illustrates how
a focus on the mode of communication, whether written or spoken, can
obscure the fact that behavior across time is similar.

The second party system emerged in the 1830s and had significant
implications for the presidency (Korzi 2004). The advent of the nomina-

tion process tied presidents more closely to their parties. The strength of political parties had consequences for governing, and "party presidential leadership was popular and democratic but not given to dramatic displays or bold action" (Korzi 2004, 29). The party system served as a constraint on popular presidential leadership at this time. This limitation is evident when comparing Jackson to some of his successors. Whereas Jackson was able to control the Democratic Party, later presidents, such as James Polk, faced a much taller task.

Growth of the Newspaper Industry

For Jackson, communication with the public became somewhat easier. Even though travel remained difficult and sometimes dangerous, changes in printing and distribution technologies began to transform the newspaper industry. Between 1810 and 1828, circulation rose from twenty-two million to sixty-eight million (more than tripling), and the number of newspapers increased from 359 to 852 (Tebbel and Watts 1985, 75).[1] During the same period, the population of the United States grew by roughly three million persons (or 42 percent).[2]

By 1833, there were twelve hundred newspapers published in the United States (Baldasty 1992, 14). The newspaper industry grew dramatically in the 1830s because of the invention of the rotary and steam-powered presses, which allowed much cheaper and quicker production. At the same time, enthusiasm for Jacksonian democracy drove popular interest in politics (Schudson 2001). The intersection of mass-based parties and partisan newspapers allowed presidents to easily and effectively reach their own party but gave them little ability to direct their messages to others (Baldasty and Rutenbeck 1988, 61).

At election time, most newspapers sponsored a candidate and were often subsidized by the candidate's party (Tebbel and Watts 1985, 75). Once a candidate became president, these newspapers served as tools for the administration to reach the public and inform partisans about the president's policy views. However, the presidential newspaper's dominance was short-lived. In 1835 James Gordon Bennett Sr. began publishing the *New York Herald*. Although the editors of newspapers like the *Herald* may have been partisans, their papers were no longer subsidized by political parties, making them independent of party influence (Tebbel and Watts 1985, 75).

As the newspaper industry expanded later in the century, it also underwent changes that proved difficult for presidents to manage. Jackson and Polk used the administration's organ with remarkable effectiveness, but later presidents struggled to do so. The influence of the president's paper declined significantly during this period before disappearing entirely during the Buchanan administration. What remained was a partisan but independent press, which provided a challenging communications environment for presidents until Lincoln was able to master the press to shape public opinion (discussed later in this chapter).

Connecting with the People

Jackson realized that the American people would be an important source of power in enacting his legislative agenda, and as a result, his administration was more connected to the public than that of any of his predecessors. Jackson was elected in 1828 with a record 57 percent of eligible voters casting ballots (Parsons 2009). This historic level of participation was a result of the Jacksonians' efforts to unite the opposition to John Quincy Adams behind the former general after Jackson's defeat in the 1824 election.

As president, Jackson linked his actions to the popular will. He also set a number of precedents in communicating with his partisans in the context of advancing his legislative agenda, including the interpretation of elections as policy mandates, the use of the veto, and the notion that the president is the representative of the people, sometimes in opposition to the other branches of government (Laracey 2002).

Jackson's connection to the people was evident at his inauguration, which was the first one attended by members of the public in addition to members of Congress and other dignitaries (Parsons 2009). Jackson appreciated the fact that he was linked to the public in a unique way, and he moved quickly to leverage that relationship to enact his agenda. Jackson wielded his popularity like a rhetorical tool to get things done. In his inaugural address on March 4, 1829, he said, "As long as our government is administered for the good of the people, and is regulated by their will the recent demonstration of public sentiment inscribes on the list of Executive duties in characters too legible to be overlooked, the task of 'reform.'" Jackson's inauguration was the first step in establishing himself as the people's representative and justifying his actions through the popular will.

Jackson expertly used his administration's newspaper to strengthen his link to the public by explicitly explaining his policies and political maneuvering. This strategy was especially useful during the most important political issue of Jackson's presidency: renewal of the National Bank charter. During the 1828 campaign and early in his administration, the *United States Telegraph* and its editor Duff Green served as Jackson's mouthpiece. However, Green was interested in one of Jackson's rivals, John C. Calhoun, which led Jackson to establish his own paper. In 1830 Jackson established the *Globe* to "provide an effective counterweight to Green in the capital" (Pollard 1947; Wilentz 2006, 359). Jackson used the *Globe* to publicize his side of the story regarding the National Bank and attempted to garner public support for his position with his written rhetoric.

From the beginning of his first term, Jackson viewed the National Bank and its supporters as hostile (Meacham 2008, 103). The president used his public communications to address the issue of the bank and build public support for his position. In his first annual message on December 8, 1829, Jackson addressed the fact that the National Bank's charter was due to expire in 1836 and that the "constitutionality and the expediency of the law creating this bank are well questioned by a large portion of our fellow citizens, and it must be admitted by all that it has failed in the great end of establishing an uniform and sound currency." Jackson addressed the issue again in his second annual message in 1830. He wrote, "The importance of the principles involved in the inquiry whether it will be proper to re-charter the Bank of the United States requires that I should again call the attention of Congress to the subject. Nothing has occurred to lessen in any degree the dangers which many of our citizens apprehend from that institution as present[ly] organized." In his third annual message, Jackson stated, "Entertaining the opinions heretofore expressed in relation to the Bank of the United States as at present organized, I felt it my duty in my former messages frankly to disclose them, in order that the attention of the Legislature and the people should be seasonably directed to that important subject." This language illustrates that presidents viewed both Congress and the public as audiences for their annual messages even in the early nineteenth century.

Though the bank's charter was not due to expire for another two years, Nicholas Biddle, president of the Second Bank of the United States, thought it would be a smart political move to try to recharter the bank in 1832. Biddle doubted that Jackson had the will to veto the bill, and if he did, Biddle hoped a veto would cost Jackson reelection (Meacham 2008, 209). Biddle was wrong on both counts. Jackson issued his now famous veto on July 10, 1832, and was reelected in November, partly on the strength of that veto (Feller 2008).

Jackson published his veto message, explaining his decision, in the *Globe*. He reasoned, "I sincerely regret that in the act before me I can perceive none of those modifications of the bank charter which are necessary, in my opinion, to make it compatible with justice, with sound policy, or with the Constitution of our country." Moreover, Jackson specifically explained that he was protecting the public at the cost of the "foreigners" and "some of our own opulent citizens."

Newspapers across the country weighed in on the issue and on the veto in particular.[3] Many published Jackson's reasons for vetoing the bank's rechartering and then added commentary by the editors. By disseminating his reasoning through the newspaper and looking for public support, Jackson enraged many of his opponents, including John C. Calhoun (Meacham 2008). In short, Jackson's veto message was "a brilliant political document, crafted for a wide circulation in order to reach over the hands of Congress, build public support, and unite the disparate Jacksonian factions opposed to the [bank]" (Wilentz 2006, 369). This description of the president's veto message is the quintessential realization of going public. Importantly, Jackson and Calhoun were fighting for supremacy within the newly constituted Democratic Party, which made Jackson's use of the newspaper much more effective than if the challenge were coming from the opposing side.[4]

The veto message also presented a challenge to the Supreme Court. Jackson wrote that he found the court's decision in *McCulloch v. Maryland* inconclusive, but more importantly, he noted that the president was "bound to interpret the laws as he understood them regardless of what the Court said" (Meacham 2008, 211). In addition to endless discussion in the newspapers, Jackson's message provoked a response from his opponents in Congress. Daniel Webster claimed the message "attacked a whole class of people," and Henry Clay likened Jackson's act to that of "a European despot" (Wilentz 2006, 371). Despite using this powerful rhetoric, bank supporters were unable to muster enough support to override the president's veto.

In October 1832 the ongoing issue prompted Jackson to travel to Kentucky, home of his chief rival on the bank issue, Henry Clay. The *Globe* reported, "Nothing certainly could evince, in a more striking manner, the personal popularity of General Jackson than the enthusiastic feeling which broke forth at Lexington, to give him a welcome. At Lexington, he was in the very heart of the Bank dominion in the West" ("From the Washington Globe" *Vermont Gazette*, October 16, 1832, 1). The paper commented on the embarrassment Clay must have felt at Jackson's reception: "It was doubtless mortifying to Mr. Clay to witness the spontaneous affection with which the General was received."

Despite the veto, the National Bank continued to be viable because federal deposits remained. Jackson viewed his reelection as a signal of

Table 2.1: Andrew Jackson and the Bank of the United States

Author	Document or Event	Date
Jackson	First annual message	December 8, 1829
Jackson	Second annual message	December 6, 1830
Jackson	Third annual message	December 6, 1831
Jackson	Veto message	July 10, 1832
Jackson	Trip to KY	October 16, 1832
Jackson	Reelection	November 1832
Jackson	Tour of MD, PA, NY, CT, MA	June 6–July 4, 1833
Jackson	Message read to cabinet on removal of federal deposits	September 18, 1833
Clay	Tour of DE, PA, NY	October 1833
Jackson	Fifth annual message	December 3, 1833
Jackson	Special message	December 12, 1833
Clay	Senate resolution seeking message to cabinet	December 1833
Jackson	Special message	February 4, 1834
Jackson	Special message	March 11, 1834
Clay	Senate censure	March 28, 1834
Jackson	Message to Senate protesting censure resolution	April 15, 1834

the public's opposition to the bank and moved more boldly to dissolve the institution. In his second inaugural address on March 4, 1833, Jackson claimed, "the will of the American people, expressed through their unsolicited suffrage, calls me before you." As the standoff between bank supporters and the Jackson administration continued, the president ordered federal deposits removed from the bank. This hostile move angered the opposition even further, eventually leading to the Senate's censure of Jackson. Table 2.1 shows important milestones in the debate regarding the National Bank and illustrates the back-and-forth maneuvering of Jackson and his opponents.

When it appeared that Congress was set to reverse Jackson's decision in 1833, Amos Kendall advised the president to withdraw the government's deposits from the bank and use the *Globe* to defend his decision

(Laracey 2002, 70; Meacham 2008, 257). Over the next six months, the *Globe* carried almost daily commentary about the bank issue, including explanations of the administration's decisions and responses to supporters of the bank (Laracey 2002, 72). In addition, the paper carried speeches made on the floor of Congress against the bank, anonymous letters from supporters, and resolutions from state legislators and party conventions that endorsed the administration's position (Laracey 2002, 72).

In the midst of this controversy, Jackson set out on a tour of New England in June 1833. His opponents in the media worried about the success of the tour and the boost it would provide to the already immensely popular president (Meacham 2008, 263). Jackson spent twenty-eight days traveling and gave about fifteen speeches (Pluta 2014). The decision to go on tour was even more significant given his chronic poor health, which made traveling difficult, painful, and even dangerous. However, even in the 1830s the president realized that being popular and providing tangible evidence of that popularity would prove advantageous in a policy debate.

The *Globe* published Jackson's directive to remove the federal government's deposits from the National Bank on September 20, 1833. A week later, Biddle made his move, calling in credits and restricting borrowing in an effort to provoke public backlash against Jackson. At this point, Jackson and Biddle agreed: "the future of the Bank was now a political question, and would be decided by public opinion as expressed in Congress" (Meacham 2008, 269). The public understood where the combatants stood on the issue and sent many petitions to Washington, "begging Jackson for relief from the economic woes Biddle was inflicting on the country" (Meacham 2008, 270). Debate flourished in newspapers across the country.

Jackson addressed the issue again on December 3, 1833, in his fifth annual message. He cited "unquestionable proof that the Bank of the United States was converted into a permanent electioneering engine" and concluded that the US Treasury should "deprive that great corporation of the support and countenance of the Government in such and use of its funds." Moreover, "at this time the efforts of the bank to control public opinion, through the distresses of some and the fears of others, are equally apparent, and, if possible, more objectionable." The president concluded the section of his message on the bank by writing, "Coming as you do, for the most part, immediately from the people and the States by election, and possessing the fullest opportunity to know their sentiments, the present Congress will be sincerely solicitous to carry into full and fair effect the will of their constituents in regard to this institution."

In a special message to Congress on December 12, Jackson not only refused to provide Congress with documents about the removal of the federal deposits but also explicitly linked his actions to the public's will and wrote, "Feeling my responsibility to the American people, I am willing upon all occasions to explain to them the grounds of my conduct." Though addressed to Congress, the *Globe* published all these documents in their entirety, and it was clear from Jackson's words and actions that both Congress and the American people were his intended audience.

Jackson's opponents in the Senate made a concerted effort to challenge the president. Clay responded to Jackson's move on December 26, 1833, with a powerful message of his own on the Senate floor. The Senate censured Jackson in March 1834 for removing the deposits from the bank. Jackson struck back on April 15, 1834, with a document titled "Protest," in which he mentioned "the people" thirty-two times. He also explicitly stated that "the President is the direct representative of the American People." The press documented, discussed, and analyzed each of these moves.

In a quintessential example of going public, Andrew Jackson sought public support in his battle with Congress over the Bank of the United States. His policy preference was maintained, and "the attack on the [bank] captured the public's imagination as proof that Jackson was the intrepid defender of the 'humble members of society'" (Wilentz 2006, 373). In addition, because of Jackson's successful use of the veto, policy and partisan purposes became important motivations behind its use in the future (Korzi 2004, 27). By successfully going public and increasing the power of the office, Jackson illustrated one of the benefits associated with participating in the competitive political environment. Jackson "made a bold bid to place himself at the absolute center of the country's life and governance, eliminating a rival by building an emotional case, repeating his point over and over again, largely through friendly newspapers, then seeking and winning vindication at the polls" (Meacham 2008, 212). Jackson's ability to communicate effectively and utilize the presidency to portray himself as the representative of the American people had consequences for presidential politics in general. After Jackson, the nation paid much more attention to presidential elections (participation reached 80 percent and remained there for most of the century). Ironically, "Jackson and the Jacksonians had made contests over the presidency, as well as the presidency itself, matter as never before, but the great surge of 1840 came on behalf of an anti-Jacksonian candidate and party pledged to curtailing presidential power" (Wilentz 2006, 515).

Jackson set new precedents in popular presidential communication, including his use of the veto to stand up for the will of the people. In doing so, Jackson communicated his policy positions to the public and asked the American people to support him. In sum, "Jackson transformed the office and its potential and made it the focus of national leadership based on boldly democratic premises" (Wilentz 2006, 525). Many subsequent presidents would follow this strategy, but none of those that immediately followed Jackson would be nearly as successful. Importantly, most of Jackson's efforts to go public were directed at members of his own party, however loosely defined at that point. One of the obstacles Jackson's successors faced was maturation of the opposition. Once the challenge became convincing Whigs of policy positions, the administration newspaper was a much less powerful tool.

Jackson was immediately followed in office by his handpicked successor, Martin Van Buren. Van Buren continued many of Jackson's policies but failed to properly gauge growing public dissatisfaction and the Whigs' effectiveness in providing an ideological alternative (Wilson 1984, 193). It was Van Buren's brilliance in organizing anti-Adams factions that had led to Jackson's election in 1828. In an ironic twist, it was the coming of age of the party system that led to Van Buren's loss in 1840. An influx of new voters allowed Whig and war hero William Henry Harrison to win the election by a narrow margin (150 to 144 electors; Wilson 1984, 207).

Becoming President: John Tyler (1841–1845)

Whig ideology suggested that William Henry Harrison would be deferential to Congress. However, when Harrison died a little more than a month into his term, Vice President John Tyler became the first person to accede to the presidency. The country debated whether Tyler would become president or whether he was simply the vice president acting as president (Chitwood 1939; Peterson 1989). The battle over the new president's title and powers took place in the newspapers, and as expected, almost all the Whig papers accepted Tyler as the president. However, former president John Quincy Adams remained skeptical (Chitwood 1939; Peterson 1989). Some Democratic papers were reluctant to use the title "president," although they mostly agreed that Tyler was entitled to the powers of the office (Dinnerstein 1962).

Tyler immediately reached out to the public to claim legitimacy and counteract concerns that he was simply the "acting" president. In a letter dated April 9, 1841, and addressed to the American people, Tyler attempted to legitimize his newly assumed position. He began by expressing his deep sympathy over the death of Harrison and mentioned that the president was usually given the opportunity to "present his countrymen an exposition of policy which will guide his inauguration in the form of an inaugural address." Given the circumstances, publishing a letter in the newspaper was the only way Tyler could reach the nation. His letter had two purposes: establish his priorities with the American people and establish his legitimacy as president. Tyler discussed the important issues of the day, including the armed forces, patronage and removal from office, public expenditures, and the currency.

Tyler faced a number of issues during his first days in office. The new president was, after all, "at heart a Democrat" (Chitwood 1939, 208). Harrison's cabinet, which Tyler felt compelled to keep intact, was filled with supporters of Henry Clay, who led the Whig Party and the Whigs in Congress (Chitwood 1939), and they expected the president to implement Whig policy. The US economy was still on shaky ground from the panics of 1837 and 1839. Clay's solution was to recharter the Bank of the United States and impose higher tariffs. However, Tyler was reluctant to follow that plan, since he had openly opposed the old bank and had even given campaign speeches against the creation of a new one (Crapol 2006, 19).

Tensions reached a boiling point in August 1841 when Tyler vetoed the bank's rechartering on the grounds that it was unconstitutional (Pollard 1947). In his veto message, Tyler laid out his reasons and plainly stated that he had "never concealed" his opposition to the bank and had been "elected by the people Vice-President of the United States." Here, Tyler clearly linked his election with a policy position he had expressed repeatedly and publicly. In the rest of the veto message, Tyler dissected the history of the National Bank and presented that history as an argument against it.

Whig congressman John Minor Botts (W-VA) published a public letter attacking Tyler's position, and the president's veto was met by protests outside the White House on the night of August 16. In response, supporters of the president gathered in front of the executive mansion the next morning to express their approval (Chitwood 1939). On August 19 Senator Clay gave a speech against the president's action, and Senator Rives (D-VA) gave a speech supporting the move. The *Madisonian* published both speeches and editorialized on August 21 that "the public will judge on the merits of each."

The newspapers followed the political drama intensely, reprinting the veto message, Clay's rejoinder, and other responses and adding their own editorial comments. Newspapers that supported the president's decision reminded readers that Tyler had opposed the bank consistently throughout his career. The president received threatening letters, and much of the Whig press was openly hostile (Pollard 1947). One line of criticism charged that since Tyler had not been elected president by the people, he could not claim to be acting in their interests (Crapol 2006). The *Madisonian* defended Tyler against these charges on August 17, claiming an "act of Providence and the choice of the People placed Mr. Tyler at the head of government."[5] Other papers, including the *Richmond Enquirer*, praised Tyler's position, writing on August 20, "it is the duty of the Representative of the people to devise the mode of keeping the public money." The Senate attempted to pass the bank bill over the president's veto on August 19 but was unsuccessful (Chitwood 1939).

Tyler's second veto caused an even harsher reaction, including assassination threats, formal expulsion from the party, and resignation of a majority of the cabinet (Peterson 1989; Zarefsky 2008; Crapol 2006). Tyler began his September 9, 1841, veto message by declaring that it was "with extreme regret" that he was "constrained" by his "duty to the Constitution" to return the bank bill to the House. Tyler claimed that the "duty [of the president] is to guard the fundamental will of the people themselves from (in this case, I admit, unintentional) change or infraction by a majority in Congress." The president then listed the specific provisions of the bill he found problematic.

As expected, the *Madisonian* defended Tyler's position throughout the summer and fall, repeatedly pointing out that the president's opinion on the bank had been consistent throughout his political career. The paper also printed letters of resignation from Tyler's cabinet. In response to these criticisms, Tyler built on strategies Jackson had used effectively during his own bank controversy, including communicating his policy positions to the public in writing. In a letter to the citizens of Kent County dated November 1841, Tyler discussed the National Bank. When the *Ohio Democrat* reprinted the letter on November 25, it claimed that the question of the National Bank had been decided, as this was seen as a statement of policy by the president.[6] Tyler wrote:

> The same opinions as to the power of Congress to charter a National Bank, which I then avowed in the presence of your fathers, and of many who still survive among you, and which, as your representative, I stren-

uously urged you in 1819, are still maintained with aiding & undiminished conviction. I was then sustained by the people of this district, with almost entire unanimity, and I therefore take leave to say, that if any of them are converts to new opinions, they might at least have grated to me, as the Chief Magistrate, bound by oath to support the constitution, the benefit of the new lights of reason, which have been shed upon them before they united with others in a spirit of unqualified denunciation.

Tyler concluded that he would continue on this path, despite the "torrents of abuse," and would place his "confidence . . . in the patriotism, discernment and intelligence of the American people."

Members of Congress, including Calvary Morris (W-OH), wrote public letters criticizing the president. Tyler responded at some length and defended himself against these attacks with letters of his own. One example, written February 10, 1842, was addressed to "his political friends in Philadelphia." In this letter, Tyler explained the difficulties he faced in being unable to broadly influence his own party. He noted that the vice president was selected "more with reference to supposed sectional or local, than to general influence." Further, "instead of being a leader," the vice president "must be a follower of party, and he is required to either be a piece of wax, to be moulded into any shape that others may please, or denunciations the loudest and boldest are in store for him." Tyler concluded, "Credit should be restored, industry reanimated, a sound currency provided through the direct exercise of Constitutional power, and the public peace observed, if the same can be accomplished without a surrender of national honor."

In an effort to gain "much-needed public exposure and to polish his tarnished image," Tyler went on tour in the spring of 1843 (Crapol 2006, 186). The tour lasted thirteen days and included seventeen speeches, and for the first time, a newspaper correspondent traveled with the president. As a follow-up to the tour, Tyler reviewed his course publicly in June 1843 (published in the *Madisonian*). Table 2.2 shows the timeline of Tyler and his vetoes.

Table 2.2: John Tyler and the Bank of the United States

Author	Document or Event	Date
Tyler	Veto message	August 16, 1841
Botts	Public letter	August 16, 1841
Tyler	Veto message	September 9, 1841
Tyler	Public letter	November 1841
Tyler	Response to Botts	May 15, 1843
Tyler	Tour	June 9–21, 1843

Although Tyler used some of the same techniques as Jackson, he was not successful. In a critical piece that appeared on September 28, 1841, the *Southern Argus* explained that Jackson had been able to hold the Democratic Party together through the bank controversy in part because of his total control of the party. Tyler had no such power over the Whig Party, according to the paper's account and his own admission. The Whigs' lack of confidence in him left Tyler virtually alone in his efforts to lead. Even if the Democrats had been open to Tyler's arguments, the structure of the newspaper environment made it very difficult to reach them.

The Administration Newspaper: James K. Polk (1845–1849) and the *Daily Union*

As detailed earlier, Andrew Jackson skillfully used his newspaper during the battle over the Bank of the United States. James K. Polk used the *Washington Daily Union* "to whip up support among members of Congress and the public for the president's programs," especially his foreign policy initiatives (Laracey 2002; Korzi 2004, 136–137). Given the importance to his ability to govern, Polk took great care in selecting the editor and the newspaper that would represent his administration.

Polk, a Jackson protégé, saw the *Union* as "his ultimate weapon against recalcitrant Democrats" (Korzi 2004, 137).[7] Because his audience was largely Democrats, the president used his newspaper to discipline members, whip up his base, and counter attacks from the opposition. For example, when English papers criticized Polk's position on Oregon expansion in his inaugural address, the *Union* vigorously supported the president's "patriotic declaration" in its May 6, 1845, edition. The paper spent the month of May publishing letters, proclamations, and supportive accounts of the president's position from around the country.[8]

Polk failed to achieve the same success as Jackson had with his newspaper, partly because the party was more divided along sectional lines; this was exacerbated by Polk's decision not to seek reelection (Appleton, Cutler, and Polk 1986; Wilentz 2006). Democrats with presidential ambitions sought to maintain distinct policy positions, including on divisive issues such as the tariff and, of course, slavery (Appleton et al. 1986, xxiii).

Because "unbiased, nonpartisan press barely existed during the second party system," Polk also went on tour in an effort to contain the "growth of anti-war sentiment in the Northeast" (Appleton et al. 1986, xvi). It may be easy to dismiss Polk's journey as simply a ceremonial one, but this would misconstrue "the young republic's conflicting concepts of the Union" and the presidency's unique potential to overcome this simmering divide (Appleton et al. 1986, xvii).

At the president's behest, journalist John Appleton joined Polk on tour and kept a journal of the trip (Appleton et al. 1986, 83). He recorded Polk's speeches, sometimes word for word and sometimes in summary, providing a contemporary view of popular presidential communication. Much of Polk's rhetoric was ceremonial in nature, as the president heaped praise on the towns and cities he visited. However, he sometimes alluded to the larger issues at stake. In a reply to the governor of Massachusetts, Polk said, "Your allusion to the Union meets my hearty response. There is an alter [*sic*] at which we may all worship. However much we may differ about local or temporary questions of policy, on the question of the Union, we are all united" (Appleton et al. 1986, 49). In Maine, Polk discussed the potential consequences if the Union were dissolved. He said, "Let the Union be dissolved, and instead of the spectacle which we now present to the world, of a united confederacy of happy and prosperous states, we shall exhibit, as the mournful fruit of dissevered councils, an extended series of petty principalities, without harmony in either, and wasting their resources, and their energies by warring among themselves" (Appleton et al. 1986, 69).

The further north the president traveled, the more he extolled the benefits of the Union. Unsurprisingly, Polk avoided discussing the hot-button issues of the day: expansion and slavery. The president was not constitutionally prohibited from doing so, but it would have been bad politics to bring up these divisive issues where sentiments for abolition and against expansion were strong. Instead, Polk took advantage of the opportunity to further the ultimate political cause: preservation of the Union.

Sectional Strife: Zachary Taylor (1849–1850), Millard Fillmore (1850–1853), Franklin Pierce (1853–1857), and James Buchanan (1857–1861)

The growing specter of slavery and sectional tension continued to take its toll on the executive's ability to exercise power as both the Democratic and the Whig Parties were badly fractured in the years before the Civil War. In 1848, when the Whigs nominated war hero General Zachary Taylor, there was great tension between the northern and southern branches of the party. Much like Polk and his efforts to overcome these tensions, Taylor went on a northern tour in 1849 to "augment his knowledge of the North's economy and needs and wishes of the citizens there" (Hamilton 1951, 224). During his travels, Taylor addressed some public policy issues, including Cuba, the tariff, and the expansion of slavery, and he took positions that were "harnessed to a strategic partisan agenda" (Ellis and Walker 2007, 249; Laracey 2002). Taylor made some strategic choices, such as beginning his tour in Pennsylvania, where the tariff was the most important political issue (Korzi 2004; Smith 1988; Eisenhower 2008, 99). However, Taylor was a terrible speaker, and this lessened the impact of his speeches (Hamilton 1951; Smith 1988). Taylor was also quite ill during the tour and was forced to return to Washington after his speech in Mercer County, Pennsylvania (Ellis and Walker 2007).

Taylor engaged with Senator Henry Clay over the issue of slavery in the new western states. The president was in a difficult position, however, since Whigs were supposed to be deferential to Congress (Laracey 2002, 92–93). All in all, Taylor proved unable to "raise public attitudes toward his administration" or to manipulate the growing power of the press (Tebbel and Watts 1985, 138).

After Taylor's untimely death in 1850, Millard Fillmore became president. He tried to build support for the Compromise of 1850 while touring the North, where antislavery sentiment was high, but his attempts to build support on both sides during the era of a partisan press proved futile (Chamberlain 1856, 155; Smith 1988, 199–200; Tebbel and Watts 1985, 144). Newspapers would remain partisan after the Civil War, but they would become independent of party (Baldasty 1992; Schudson 2001).

Presidents had difficulty reaching the people and leading public opinion through newspapers in part because the administration newspaper was in decline. As newspapers that were not attached to the administration proliferated, the president's ability to control and disseminate the news became increasingly difficult (Baldasty 1992; Schudson 2001). This problem was exacerbated because both parties were badly fractured over the issue of slavery (Holt 2003). Presidents from Zachary Taylor through James Buchanan faced an increasingly difficult environment that they were unprepared to navigate.

Despite these challenges, even some seemingly weak presidents exhibited certain aspects of rhetorical leadership that were becoming more important. Both Franklin Pierce and James Buchanan "drew upon popular authority to bolster their leadership claims" and endorsed the concept of a mandate in their electoral victories (Bimes and Mulroy 2004, 147). With the exception of Buchanan, all the presidents in this period went on speaking tours in an attempt to connect with the people (Pluta 2014). However, these presidents' failure to positively influence "public attitudes

toward [their] administrations" complicated their ability to have successful presidencies (Tebbel and Watts 1985, 138).

The administration newspaper was fatally weakened in March 1861
when Congress established the US Government Printing Office. This de-
partment, with 350 federal workers, assumed responsibility for publishing most of the nation's executive, legislative, and judicial records. In the
past, the administration's newspaper would have received these lucrative
government printing orders. Abraham Lincoln further upended the old
order by "doling out information to the more widely read Washington
dailies, one story at a time" (Holzer 2014, 308). Lincoln's strategy was to
use the DC newspapers "selectively and informally—occasionally pitting
one against the other in quest of the best coverage" (Holzer 2014, 308).
This practice of spreading information among multiple outlets effectively
ended the presidential newspaper.

Interlude: Abraham Lincoln (1861–1865)

Lincoln does not fit neatly into either the "going partisan" era or the "going regional" era covered in the next chapter. Of course, his status as the
only president in the nation's history to preside over a civil war is as good
an explanation as any. However, Lincoln also understood the media environment in which he operated, and this insight allowed him to expertly
and uniquely use the press to his advantage to shape public opinion.

After a number of ineffective presidents, Lincoln proved to be a
master of press relations, and this ability helped him guide the nation
through a bloody civil war. Unlike Jackson, Lincoln could not claim a
mandate,[9] having been elected with only 40 percent of the popular vote.
Moreover, he now led a badly divided nation on the precipice of civil war.
Lincoln expertly used newspapers to lead public opinion throughout the
war effort (Holzer 2014).

The media environment of the 1860s was different from the era of the
presidential newspaper. While the press remained partisan, powerful edi-

tors took center stage, "reaching larger audiences than ever before, largely independent of political subsidy as a whole. They [newspapers] offered politicians not a fanatical, screaming party press as in the past but a national debating platform" (Tebbel and Watts 1985, 168).

The Civil War had a profound impact on the press, including a significant increase in daily circulation (Tebbel and Watts 1985). Although greater circulation meant that more citizens would receive his message, the Civil War complicated Lincoln's relationship with the press. One point of tension was how much freedom the press should be allowed. Lincoln tried to be accessible to the press and answered questions in what might be considered an early form of the press conference (Tebbel and Watts 1985, 183). However, Lincoln also suppressed almost three hundred Democratic newspapers that were sympathetic to the Confederacy (Bulla 2009).

During the Civil War, Lincoln employed a number of strategies to deal with the press and to shape public opinion. In addition to selecting certain newspapers to disseminate information, he used newspaper leaks to preview policy proclamations and prepare the public for important announcements. Lincoln also engaged in correspondence with newspaper editors. Few of these "appeals to the people through the press ever earned such widespread circulation, commentary or lasting fame" (Holzer 2014, 200). However, these letters served an important purpose: they allowed Lincoln to slowly introduce a policy, gauge public reaction, and make a case to the people (Holzer 2014).

Emancipation was the most delicate undertaking of Lincoln's political career. For more than a year, he slowly prepared the American public for this monumental moment, making expert use of the newspaper. On August 22, 1862, the president wrote a letter to Horace Greeley, editor of the *New York Tribune*, that carefully described Lincoln's position on slavery and the Union. This correspondence was the last in a series of strategic communications meant to ensure that most Americans would accept emancipation (Holzer 2014).

Lincoln, like a number of his predecessors, replied to citizen groups and other entities to communicate his policy preferences. Other letters covered important issues such as Lincoln's arbitrary arrests of alleged conspirators, the conduct of the war, the draft in New York State, and other problems facing the president and the country (Laracey 2002, 111). Lincoln also allowed "interviews" with him to be discussed and published. These interviews were often conversations with members of Congress or other political figures and covered critical political topics. In two examples of conversations with members of Congress from Kentucky (published in the *Maysville Weekly*, October 13, 1864, and the *Alexandria Gazette*, November 25, 1862), the president discussed at length the question of emancipation and the arrest of Colonel Wolford. In both cases, Lincoln was able to convey his position on important issues to the public through the newspaper.

Lincoln spent a lifetime observing and working with the press. Throughout his career, Lincoln used the press as a political tool, and at one point he even owned a newspaper (Holzer 2014). It was this experience that allowed him to understand and utilize the press to his greatest advantage, given the difficult circumstances. In commenting on Lincoln's prowess with the press and the people, Chauncey M. Depew offered a quote from the president:

> "Yes, all the newspapers will publish my letter, and so will Greeley. The next day he will take a line and comment upon it, and he will keep it up, in that way, until at the end of three weeks, I will be convicted out of my own mouth of all things which he charges against me. No man, whether he be private citizen or president of the U.S., can successfully carry on a controversy with a great newspaper, and escape destruction unless he owns a newspaper equally great with a circulation in the same neighborhood" (Depew 1889, 436)

Despite his prowess as an orator, Lincoln often relied on written communications. Instead of "time-consuming public speeches," Lincoln transformed the "public letter into a weapon of mass communication."

Lincoln was careful to send his letters to various outlets, including ones that disagreed with him (Holzer 2014, 448). Here, Lincoln was building on the successful strategies of his predecessors but adapting to an evolving media environment.

Lincoln solved what would become an enduring problem for American presidents that had not existed in the era of administration newspapers. Public support has always been an essential element of the president's power, but cultivating that support without press interference can be difficult. With the administration newspaper, presidents had a direct conduit to the people, or at least to their fellow partisans. Without that organ, communicating directly with the public became more difficult. Moreover, the partisan nature of the press, which endured until the early twentieth century, continued to limit the persuadable public.

Conclusion

Many nineteenth-century presidents understood that a relationship with the public was important, and they utilized written rhetoric because technological constraints and the partisan media made it the most practical and politically expedient choice. Andrew Jackson, in particular, was able to leverage the presidential newspaper to bring his case against the National Bank directly to the public. Jackson's ability to harness public opinion on this important issue allowed him to not only win reelection but also overcome opposition in Congress. Jackson was successful, in part, because he was feuding with other Democrats at a time when partisanship in the electorate was just taking hold. Jackson was able to reach those whom he intended to persuade.

Jackson's successors, including Tyler and Polk, were not as fortunate. John Tyler attempted to use written public communications to assert his legitimacy and ensure that his policy preferences were maintained. However, Tyler's inability to garner support from the Whig Party made this task difficult. Importantly, the partisan newspaper system prevented presidents from reaching beyond their own supporters. James Polk used his public communications to motivate his partisans, while reaching detractors continued to be difficult because of the partisan press and limited travel capabilities. Lincoln, in contrast, presented an enduring lesson: presidents who are able to communicate effectively with the public, regardless of the structural constraints of the media, have an important advantage in pursuing popular support for their agenda.

3

Going Regional: Andrew Johnson to
Benjamin Harrison, 1866–1893

Presidents in the post–Civil War period faced the enormously difficult task
of uniting the country after a devastating war. Contention over who would be
included in American democracy made this project even more arduous. Although the era began with an expansion in the franchise, with all men having
the right to vote, this universal male enfranchisement would be short-lived.
The next phase of popular presidential communication, which I call
"going regional," saw the first significant increase in spoken communication with the public, as presidents leveraged the complex process of industrialization to travel farther and more safely than ever before. However,
this trend toward increased speech was not entirely consistent, suggesting
that technology was not the only variable at play. This chapter investigates
how brief universal male enfranchisement, strong political parties with
regional components, a partisan but independent newspaper industry,
and rapid technological innovation led to changes in presidential rhetoric.

Frequency of Spoken Popular Presidential Communication

American presidents' increasing use of speech to communicate with the
public has been the subject of scholarly debate for the last forty years.

Average Spoken Popular Presidential Communication per Year: Washington to Trump

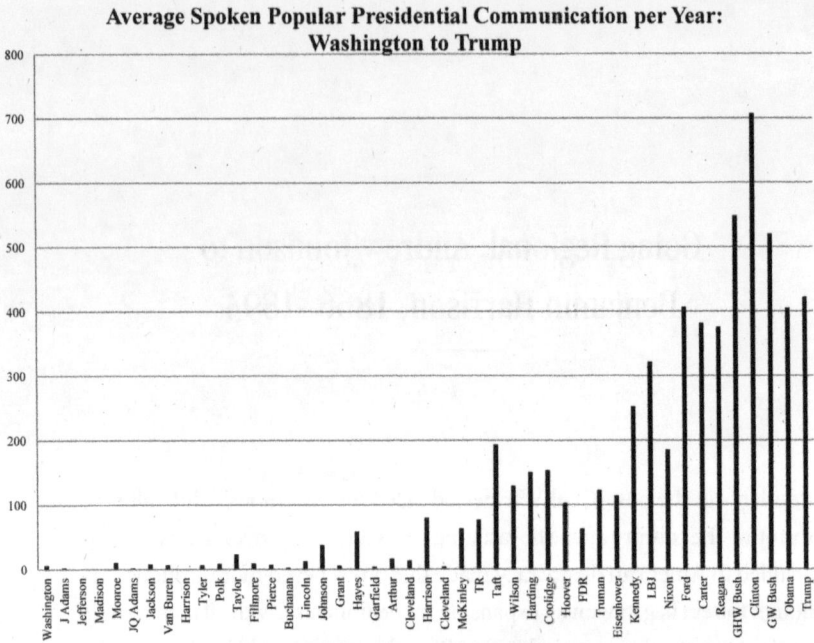

Figure 3.1. Frequency of spoken presidential communication per year, by president: Washington through Trump. (Source: author's data)

Topics of interest include the causes of this greater frequency of speech, the usefulness of such speech, and its potentially deleterious effects on democratic discourse (Tulis 1987; Kernell [1986] 1997; Edwards 2006; Pluta 2015). This chapter illustrates that the increase in speech making began much earlier than is often recognized and that the change was primarily the product of technological innovation, attempts to navigate an evolving media environment, and political incentives to develop a relationship with the public.

For the first time, easier travel enabled presidents to expand the persuadable public. Newspapers remained partisan, so reaching the opposition was difficult, especially because opposing newspapers often included commentary about the president's statement or provided an "alternative" account of events. However, as the railroad made travel quicker and safer, presidents could reach more people without an intermediary.

A graph of the frequency of popular presidential communication per year for each president (from Washington through Trump) helps guide this chapter and allows me to begin by describing the data (figure 3.1). As figure 3.1 indicates, the first significant increase in spoken popular presidential communication occurred among the post–Civil War presidents, making this a natural starting point for an exploration into the causes of this increase. I begin by charting the growth of the railroad, the key technological innovation of the mid-nineteenth century that influenced presidential communications.[1] I look closely at Andrew Johnson (1865–1869), Rutherford B. Hayes (1877–1881), and Benjamin Harrison (1889–1893), who made significantly more speeches per year than their predecessors. I also examine Chester Arthur (1881–1885) and Grover Cleveland (1885–1889, 1893–1897), who defied the tendency toward more spoken rhetoric, even though their totals were in line with the overall trend.

Incentives for Spoken Communication

Political parties were strong throughout most of this period, but toward the end of the nineteenth century, regional disagreements and progressive reforms began to weaken parties' grip on the electorate. The Republican Party seemed dominant, losing only one presidential election between 1865 and 1890; however, the reality was that elections at the national level were tightly contested, which encouraged presidents to speak to the people. Rapid technological innovation, including the railroad, presented presidents with new opportunities to reach the public.

By the time of Reconstruction, the newspaper industry had undergone significant changes. Most newspapers still had partisan inclinations (Ryfe 2005), but they no longer depended on political parties for subsidies and could therefore operate largely independently (Laracey 2002; Holzer 2014). Printing materials were cheaper, the audience had grown substantially, and an independent news media was overtaking the partisan press (Ryfe 2005). Between 1870 and 1890, circulation rose by 222 percent (Cornwell 1979). This enormous growth in circulation led to an increase in advertisements, which made newspapers more profitable and changed the industry's purpose from providing a public service to operating as a business (Cornwell 1979).

As circulation grew, so did the influence, power, and independence of the press (Tebbel and Watts 1985; Ryfe 2005). A professionalizing and growing industry presented new challenges for presidents. When President Grover Cleveland got married in 1886, his honeymoon caused a media frenzy. In an effort to control the madness, Cleveland hired Daniel Lamont to serve as press secretary during the trip. In 1893, during his second term, Cleveland employed George B. Cortelyou as confidential stenographer. Cortelyou functioned as a press liaison and continued in this capacity during the McKinley administration. The White House beat reporter was established during Cleveland's second term (Nelson 1998).

Technological Innovation: The Railroad

The railroad was hardly the only technological innovation of the nineteenth century, but it was one of the most visible. Beyond changing the way Americans traveled, the railroad figured in many of the critical political and economic conflicts of the late 1800s and early 1900s (White 2011). Unlike some of the other important but less obvious innovations, the railroad directly affected the president's ability to reach the public and provided a way to circumvent the partisan newspaper environment. With this in mind, I treat the growth of the railroad both as a proxy for the myriad innovations in travel and communications in the mid to late nineteenth century and as a critical development in its own right.[2]

For many Americans, the second half of the nineteenth century was defined by the railroad. Though the first rails were laid in the 1830s, railroad construction did not take off until after the Civil War. By 1865, the

**The Frequency of Popular Presidential Communication
Compared to Railroad Miles per Year:
Jackson to Coolidge**

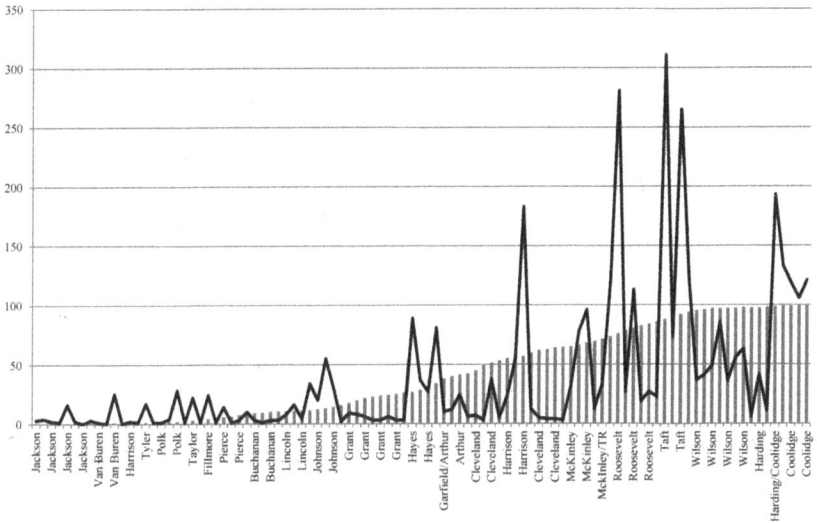

Figure 3.2. Frequency of spoken presidential communication compared to percentage of total railroad miles in existence per year: Jackson through Coolidge. (Source: US Census 1960)

United States had 35,000 miles of railroad, compared with only 9,000 in 1850. Growth exploded over the next half century. There were 92,147 miles of railroad in 1880 and almost double that, 163,355 miles, ten years later (US Census 1960).[3] More importantly, the first transcontinental railroad was completed in May 1869 (White 2011). This dramatic increase in passenger miles also meant that infrastructure, such as train cars and amenities along the way, also improved. Simply put, traveling by train became safer and more comfortable (White 2011).

The railroad not only encouraged presidents to speak rather than write to the people; it also encouraged them to do so more frequently. Figure 3.2 shows the frequency of spoken presidential communication compared to the percentage of total railroad miles in existence per year

Table 3.1: Presidential Tours: Rutherford B. Hayes through Benjamin Harrison (1877–1893)

President (Party)/ Dates	States Visited	Number of Days	Number of Speeches	Themes
Hayes (R)				
June 26–29, 1877	CT, MA, RI	3	12	Ceremonial speeches
August 16–24, 1877	VT, NH, MA	8	24	National unity, Constitution
September 7–25, 1877	OH, KY, TN, GA, VA	18	32	Reconciliation, education
September 4–24, 1878	WI, MN, IL, OH, PA	21	20	Specie payments, economy
September 9– October 18, 1879	OH, IL, KS, MO	39	25	Specie payments, economy
August 26– November 6, 1880[a]	IA, IL, WY, UT, NV, CA, OR, WA[b], AZ[b], NM[b], KS	72	71	National unity, economy, education, currency
Arthur (R)[c]				
June 29– September 6, 1883[d]	NJ, KY, IN, IL, PA	40	17	Ceremonial speeches
Cleveland (D)				
September 30– October 22, 1887	MD, PA, MO, NE, IA, IL, WI, MN, TN, GA, AL	23	20	National unity
Harrison (R)				
August 21–23, 1889[e]	IN, OH	3	15	Ceremonial speeches
October 6–13, 1890	OH, IL, IN, MO, OH	7	42	National unity, education, prosperity

April 14–May 15, 1891	VA, TN, GA, AL, AR, MS[f], TX, NM[b], AZ[b], CA, OR, WA, ID, UT, CO, NE, IA, IN, OH, PA	31	138	Economic diversification, reunion, supremacy of law
August 18–28, 1891	NY, VT	11	30	Ceremonial speeches

[a]These are the days the president was absent from Washington. However, he spent August 26–September 6 in Ohio. Hayes left Ohio on September 6 for the Midwest and the West Coast (Deacon 2011).

[b]Territories at the time of the president's visit.

[c]Tulis (1987) attributes one tour to Arthur. I am assuming this is the one because of the tone of the coverage in contemporary newspapers. On other occasions, Arthur left Washington and made ceremonial speeches along the way, but these were often referred to as "trips."

[d]Arthur spent August 3–September 5 in Yellowstone Park on vacation (Howe 1934, 248), so those days are not included in the total days on tour.

[e]After the tour, the president returned to his summer retreat in Deer Park, Maryland (*Chicago Tribune*, August 24, 1889, 11).

[f]In Mississippi, Harrison passed through a number of towns but gave no speeches (Frantz 2011, 58).

from Jackson through Coolidge.[4] Although presidents after Coolidge used the railroad to tour and campaign, the railroad was no longer expanding, so it could not be responsible for any additional growth in the frequency of communication.

The effect of the railroad is evident when looking at the amount of speaking that Rutherford B. Hayes and Benjamin Harrison did on tour. These presidents crisscrossed the country by train and spoke from station platforms to large crowds. (William McKinley and Theodore Roosevelt also toured extensively and are discussed at length in the next chapter.) This pace of travel was impossible before the railroad, and it allowed presidents to get out to the people more easily than ever before. Table 3.1 shows how often Hayes and Harrison spoke on tour, where they traveled, and the topics they addressed. These topics ranged from national unity (very important in the aftermath of the Civil War) to specie payments—a critical economic policy at the time. Some of the remarks were ceremonial greetings or replies, but these presidents were not afraid to discuss policy with the public. Hayes gave at least 184 speeches and Harrison made at least 225 speeches while on tour during their respective years in office.

All these Republican presidents had strong political incentives to tour the country and speak to the American people. In the wake of the Civil War and Reconstruction, the Republican Party was trying to reconstitute itself in the South, and the railroad allowed presidents to take their messages across the rapidly expanding nation. Every Republican president from Hayes through Taft traveled to the South, but they had to tread carefully as they tried to maintain a delicate balance between expanding the reach of the Republican Party and fulfilling promises to African Americans on civil rights. This was especially true of Hayes and Harrison, who were Civil War veterans. By the time Taft was president, the idea of preserving Black rights had largely been abandoned, and Taft began "actively campaigning for himself in the states of the former Confederacy" (Frantz 2011, 6).

Hayes was the first president to reach the West Coast, and Harrison is often credited with taking the first national tour. As the United States began to emerge on the world stage, McKinley traveled extensively in support of the Spanish-American War, and Roosevelt became the first president to travel outside the country when he went to the Panama Canal Zone in November 1906 (Ellis 2008; Frantz 2011; Pluta 2014). Political circumstances varied for these four men. Hayes and Harrison served during times of razor-thin electoral margins, and both men won in the Electoral College despite losing the popular vote. The situation was particularly perilous for Hayes, whose election was highly contentious and seen as illegitimate by some (Vazanno 2006). Moreover, Hayes faced pressures from within his own party because he refused to dole out political plums (Calhoun 2010).

McKinley won convincingly in 1896, ending the era of closely contested elections. However, participation in American politics began to drop during this period, in part as a reaction to Gilded Age politics, and in part because of the rise of other forms of entertainment and interest. Progressive reforms weakened political parties and encouraged presidents to take a more active role in campaigning and agenda setting (Gamm and Smith 1998; Klinghard 2010). Because of waning public interest, the president had to be more creative and insistent as he tried to reach and engage the people (Calhoun 2010, 180). These political circumstances contributed to increasingly frequent speeches through the early part of the twentieth century.

The Price of Going Public? Andrew Johnson (1865–1869)

Andrew Johnson was the first president to significantly increase his speech making, and he is often cited as an example of the perils of public rhetoric. Johnson gave at least 113 spoken remarks, almost double that of Abraham Lincoln, who gave only 62 speeches during his time in office. Through the lens of the persuadable public, Johnson illustrates how both the audience (i.e., who in the public is actually persuadable) and the media environment are critical to the success of presidential communication strategies. The railroad presented Johnson with the opportunity to reach the public; however, both the strength of political parties and the media environment constrained him in ways he failed to consider.

Johnson faced many obstacles when he became president after Lincoln's assassination, including an increasing hostile Congress. He lacked Lincoln's skill at harnessing and utilizing public opinion to achieve his own legislative ends. Johnson failed to learn two important lessons from Lincoln's dealings with the press: avoid public statements that could be used against him, and avoid unscripted situations where he might say the wrong thing (Laracey 2002, 116).

As president, Johnson violated both these caveats in 1866 when he set out on a tour to gain public support for presidential Reconstruction. Johnson needed to garner support because his opponents, the Radical Republicans, held a two-thirds majority in Congress and could block all his policy initiatives. The president hoped to convince voters in the East and Midwest to elect representatives who would vote to admit southern representatives to Congress and therefore allow his agenda to move forward (Phifer 1952, 4–6).

Scholars often portray this tour as unsuccessful because of Johnson's willingness to discuss policy with the public. In fact, Tulis (1987) uses Johnson to illustrate the perils of a nineteenth-century president discussing policy with the public. In contrast, I find that Johnson's tour was problematic because of the fragmented, partisan press and the president's own behavior, as opposed to the violation of a widely held constitutional norm.[5]

Despite the significant growth of the railroad, which meant that Johnson could travel farther, faster, and more safely than his predecessors, he still faced obstacles in reaching the people. In part, the president's naïveté about the partisan nature of the press and the lack of an administration organ made it unlikely that his message would reach the public as he intended (Crook and Gerry 1910; Phifer 1952). Johnson's inability to control his temper or his drinking compounded these problems (Ellis 2008; Browne 2008).

Gideon Welles, a member of Johnson's cabinet, understood the situation and counseled the president against touring. Secretary Welles was concerned for two reasons: first, he feared that Johnson would encounter deeply partisan and hostile crowds, and second, he worried that the press would twist Johnson's words, leading to a loss of public support. Johnson ignored this sage advice, given that speech making had been effective for the president in the past in Tennessee and on the campaign trail (Welles 1911; Phifer 1952). Johnson was a powerful orator who was well known for his ability to "identify with the people in simple but powerful language (Browne 2008, 205). However, as Colonel William H. Crook put it, "Mr. Johnson's manner in delivering public speeches was one which could not

be translated into newspaper language" (Crook and Gerry 1910, 106). Ultimately, Johnson's comparison to his earlier experiences was not applica-
ble, in part because there were fewer newspapers in Tennessee and thus
fewer opportunities to distort his speeches (Welles 1911).

Data and Methods

For Andrew Johnson's tour, I searched the Chronicling of America database and the *New York Times*. I used the search terms "president" and
"tour" and used the date range August 23 (the first day an article about
the president's impending trip appeared) to October 15, 1866. I focused
on specific newspapers: *New Orleans Daily Crescent* (supportive of Johnson), *Cleveland Daily Leader* (critical of Johnson), *New York Herald* (supportive), *Chicago Tribune* (critical), and *New York Tribune* (critical). This
search returned 193 results.[6] I also searched the *New York Times*, which
was supportive of Johnson. The *New York Times* search produced 180 hits
and 41 articles that addressed the president and his swing around the
country directly.[7] See table 3.2 for a list of newspapers I consulted and
short summaries of the articles, including whether the article was objective, critical of the president, or supportive of him. Articles that failed to
discuss the tour and the president were excluded from the analysis.

In coding the articles, I considered reports of any opposition Johnson faced and how the crowds and Johnson's speeches were described.
The nature of the partisan press made these characterizations relatively
straightforward (and to some degree predictable, as newspapers tended
to adhere closely to their chosen side). Many articles covered the same
general information. I paid special attention to articles that defied expectations on tone. As table 3.2 shows, there were only four articles that fell
into this category (highlighted in boldface).

As might be expected, a number of the early reports about the tour
were objective. The articles detailed who would accompany the president
and where the traveling party would stop.[8] However, as soon as contro-

Table 3.2: Press Coverage of Andrew Johnson's 1866 Tour

Topic	Article, Newspaper,[a] Date, Tone[b]
Party accompanying the president and logistics of tour	"Washington News," *NYT*, August 23, objective
	"Washington News," *NYT*, August 24, objective
	"Washington News," *NYT*, August 25, objective
Arrangements in Philadelphia	"Local Intelligence" *NYT*, August 26, objective
	"The Presidential Tour," *NYT*, August 27, objective
Trip to Baltimore (August 28)	"Washington News," *NYT*, August 27, objective
	"The Presidential Tour," *NY Herald*, August 27, supportive
	"The Presidential Trip," *NY Tribune*, August 27, supportive
	"Washington News," *Cleveland Daily Leader*, August 28, objective
	"The Presidential Tour," *Cleveland Daily Leader*, August 28, objective
	"The President's Tour," August 28, *New Orleans Daily Crescent*, objective
	"Andrew Johnson: Preparation for Tour," *NYT*, August 28, objective
	"The President's Electioneering Tour," *Chicago Tribune*, August 28, critical
	"The Presidential Tour," *NY Herald*, August 28, supportive
	"The Arrangements," *NYT*, August 29, supportive
Arrival in Baltimore (August 28)	"Latest News [reprinted speech]," *Cleveland Daily Leader*, August 29, objective
Arrival in Philadelphia	"The President's Electioneering Tour," *Chicago Tribune*, August 29, critical
	"The President's Tour," *New Orleans Daily Crescent*, August 29, supportive
	"The Tour," *NY Herald*, August 29, supportive
	"President Johnson," *NYT*, August 30, supportive
Arrival in New York City	"The Presidential Tour," *Cleveland Daily Leader*, August 30, objective
Speech at Delmonico's	"The Presidential Tour," *New Orleans Daily Crescent*, August 30, supportive

Upstate NY (Albany, Auburn, West Point)	"The President's Electioneering Tour," *Chicago Tribune*, August 30, critical "The President's Reception in New York," *NY Herald*, August 31, supportive "President Johnson," *NYT*, August 31, supportive "The Presidential Tour," *Cleveland Daily Leader*, August 31, objective "The Tour," *NY Herald*, August 31, supportive **"The President's Electioneering Tour," *Chicago Tribune*, August 31, supportive** "The Presidential Tour," *New Orleans Daily Crescent*, September 1, objective "President Johnson," *NYT*, September 1, supportive
Niagara Falls–Cleveland	"President Johnson," *NYT*, September 2, supportive "The Presidential Tour," *NY Herald*, September 2, supportive "The Tour [reprinted speech]," *NY Herald*, September 2, objective **"The President's Tour," *NY Tribune*, September 3, supportive** "The President's Tour," *New Orleans Daily Crescent*, September 3, supportive "The President's Tour," *NYT*, September 3, supportive "The Liberal Republicans," *NYT*, September 3, supportive "Presidential Tour," *NY Herald*, September 3, supportive "The Evening Post," *NYT*, September 3, supportive "The President's Tour," *NYT*, September 4, supportive "The President's Tour," *New Orleans Daily Crescent*, September 4, supportive "The President's Electioneering Tour," *Chicago Tribune*, September 4, critical "The Presidential Tour," *NY Herald*, September 4, supportive
Cleveland–Detroit	"The Presidential Tour," *New Orleans Daily Crescent*, September 5, supportive

(continued on the next page)

Table 3.2: *Continued*

Topic	Article, Newspaper,[a] Date, Tone[b]
Michigan	"The Presidential Tour," *New Orleans Daily Crescent*, September 6, supportive
Springfield–St. Louis	"The President's Electioneering Tour," *Chicago Tribune*, September 8, critical
	"St. Louis," *NYT*, September 8, objective
	"The Tour," *NY Herald*, September 9, supportive
	"The President's Tour," *NYT*, September 9, objective
	"The President's Trip," *NY Tribune*, September 10, supportive
	"The Presidential Tour," *New Orleans Daily Crescent*, September 10, supportive
	"The President's Electioneering Tour," *Chicago Tribune*, September 10, critical
President going south	"The President in the South," *NYT*, September 10, objective
	"Political Affairs," *NYT*, September 10, objective
	"President Johnson," *New Orleans Daily Crescent*, September 13, supportive
St. Louis–Terre Haute	"The President's Tour," *NYT*, September 11, objective
Arrival in Indianapolis	"Rich and Rare," *Chicago Tribune*, September 11, critical
	"The Radical Rise at Indianapolis—What's Next," *NY Herald*, September 12, supportive
	"The President's Tour," *NY Tribune*, September 12, objective
	"Presidential Tour," *New Orleans Daily Crescent*, September 12, supportive
Jeffersonville–Vienna	"The President's Tour," *NYT*, September 12, objective
Cincinnati	"The Tour," *NY Herald*, September 13, supportive
	"The Presidential Tour," *New Orleans Daily Crescent*, September 13, supportive
Eastern Ohio and western Pennsylvania	"The President's Tour," *NYT*, September 14, objective
	"The Tour," *NY Herald*, September 14, supportive

Tour generally	"The Presidential Tour," *New Orleans Daily Crescent*, September 14, supportive "The President's Tour," *NYT*, September 15, objective "The President among the People," *NYT*, August 30, supportive "I Am No Politician," *NY Herald*, September 14, supportive "President & Congress," *Chicago Tribune*, September 18, critical "The President's Tour," NY Herald, September 26, supportive **"The President & Congress," *NY Herald*, October 12, critical**
Return to DC	"National Respectability," *NY Herald*, October 13, supportive "From Washington," *NYT*, September 15, supportive "The President's Tour," *NYT*, September 16, objective "The Presidential Tour," *New Orleans Daily Crescent*, September 18, supportive

[a]The *New York Times* (*NYT*), *New York Herald*, and *New Orleans Daily Crescent* were generally supportive of the president.

[b]The tone of the articles was coded as supportive of Johnson, critical of Johnson, or objective. The four articles in boldface indicate a tone that defied expectations.

versy emerged in Philadelphia, the newspapers' partisan leanings became clear. The papers colored their coverage of the president's tour, adding editorial comments that either supported or criticized Johnson. Their partisan nature became more obvious when events were controversial. Most of the articles appeared while the president was actually on tour, although commentary continued, especially in the local papers, for weeks thereafter.

Johnson on Tour

The tour began on the morning of August 28, 1866, as the presidential train left Washington for Laurel, Maryland. At first, Welles's concerns seemed misplaced, as even editors who were opposed to Johnson presented objective (as opposed to critical) accounts of his tour. These early articles described the president and his traveling party, which included members of his cabinet, military heroes, and the press (Phifer 1952). The Associated Press noted "enthusiastic crowds" as Johnson left Washington, DC. He was well received in New York, and his speech at Delmonico's was reportedly a success, as noted even by those papers that were generally hostile to Johnson.[9]

However, there were disparities in how the tour was depicted. The August 30 edition of the *New York Herald*, a newspaper supportive of the president, described Johnson's tour as "an event as important as it is remarkable in the political history of this country. It is certainly the most remarkable Presidential tour we have had since the time of Washington, in regard to the distinguished men of this travelling party." This article described Johnson as a "patriot" who, "since his call to the Presidency, has been as magnanimous and sagacious in behalf of restoration and reconciliation between the North and South as he was before resolute and vigorous in the work of suppressing the rebellion." In another article published on September 3, the *New York Herald* described "practical common-sense speeches of President Johnson" that "day after day are eagerly listened to by those whom be addresses, and carefully read by the people of the whole country." The *Herald* predicted that Johnson's speeches "will have an unbounded influence on public opinion. We confidently look forward, as the result of all those movements, to the extinguishment of the radical republicans as a political power, and to the election of the next Congress of men who are opposed to all destructive principles and in favor of immediate, complete and unconditional return of our Southern brethren into the great national family."

In stark contrast, the *Cleveland Daily Leader* wrote on August 30 that

Johnson's speeches were unlikely to "contain anything new or original" and "consequently they will possess no particular importance." Moreover, the newspaper speculated that if Johnson were "not so imperviously wrapped up in self-conceit and obstinacy; the trip might be the means of accomplishing great good." The article concluded that because the president hears only his own partisans, he will "return to Washington as neither a wisrer [*sic*] or better man."

The tour became more contentious as it moved west. Journalists retreated firmly to their partisan corners and provided different accounts of the events. For example, as the tour moved through Illinois, the September 8 edition of the *Chicago Tribune* described a "very quiet crowd, consisting almost entirely of Copperheads," and noted that at a number of stops the crowds had come "to see Grant" and called for the general to make an appearance when the president tried to speak. Meanwhile, on September 10 the *New Orleans Daily Crescent* remarked on the "demonstrations," which were of the "most enthusiastic character," and noted that "at Auburn, Chatham and Monticello large crowds gathered and cheered the President in the heartiest manner." When the crowds were hostile, the *New York Times* blamed the radicals for disrupting and insulting the president, while the *New York Tribune* accused Johnson of sparking protests with his inappropriate behavior.

Johnson did little to help himself. He was unable to ignore hecklers, especially as crowds grew more hostile in Lincoln's home state of Illinois. Johnson attacked members of Congress in response to catcalls from the public. His speeches in Cleveland and St. Louis included numerous interruptions and sparring with unfriendly spectators (Crook and Gerry 1910; Phifer 1952). Unsurprisingly, these two speeches were the subject of questioning at Johnson's 1867 impeachment trial—not because they included policy talk but because of the president's harangues against members of Congress. Perhaps most memorably in Cleveland, Johnson responded to a harasser by saying, "Why don't you hang Thad Stevens and Wendell Phillips" (Crook and Gerry 1910; Supplement to *Congressional Globe* 1868, 111–113).

Citizens had vastly different understandings of the president's tour, depending on which account they read. This media environment made it difficult for Johnson to cultivate a relationship with the public. A parallel can be drawn to the early twenty-first century, when the internet and social media led to a discursive and highly polarized media environment in which all presidential actions were interpreted through a partisan lens.

Johnson's tour was an attempt to reach the public directly without the media as an intermediary. Previous presidents had been able to do this through the administration newspaper, but no such tool existed in 1865. Johnson's desire for unfettered access to the American public was hardly unique. In fact, the desire to reach the people without interference has been and continues to be an important goal of popular presidential communication. Again, the internet and social media provide a current example.

Interviews

Presidents in this era began to explore other avenues of reaching the public, beyond touring. One approach was giving interviews to newspaper correspondents. Despite Johnson's failure to harness public opinion on tour, he tried to reach the people through newspaper interviews published between October 1865 and May 1868. These interviews centered primarily on the president's battle with Congress over Reconstruction (Pollard 1947). Table 3.3 lists these interviews, the newspapers in which they first appeared, and the topics discussed.[10]

As might be expected, the president gave interviews to friendly newspapers, and these interviews were then reprinted nationally. These conversations often lasted for a few hours and involved many questions that the president willingly answered. Johnson linked his legitimacy to his election by the people and discussed Reconstruction and his policies more generally (Pollard 1947). In the *New York Times*, reporters described how the media environment hindered Johnson: "The President's opinions, especially with reference to the freedmen, have been so willfully

Table 3.3: Andrew Johnson Interviews[a]

Date	Newspaper	Topic
October 31, 1865	*Franklin Repository*	Freedmen, southern states
February 20, 1867	*New York Citizen*	Reconstruction
July 21, 1867	*Cincinnati Commercial*	Impeachment
December 31, 1867	*Cincinnati Commercial*	Removal power, impeachment
January 17, 1868	*New York World*	Removal power, impeachment
January 21, 1868	*New York World*	Reconstruction
February 9, 1868	*Cincinnati Commercial*	Removal of Sheridan, Reconstruction, president's policy
February 22, 1868	*New York Herald*	General politics, action of Congress
March 9, 1968	*New York World*	Conversation with Grant, impeachment
March 29 and April 2, 1868	*Cincinnati Commercial*	Impeachment
May 10, 1868	*Boston Post*	Impeachment vote

[a]This list of interviews is provided in Pollard (1947, 414). I have all these interviews in my data set, although some might be republished versions (if the original newspaper has not been digitized).

misrepresented in the radical press of this country and his general policy toward the Southern States has been exposed to so much unjustifiable perversion that Mr. Johnson's own explanations on both these subjects may have some weight even with those who are most embittered against him" ("American Topics," May 14, 1866, 1).

Despite his attempts, Johnson was unable to rally the people to his side for at least two reasons. First, the partisan press distorted his words and kept Johnson's message from reaching anyone but his own partisans. Second, Johnson's outlandish behavior was seen as unpresidential by a large segment of the population. The president's efforts to reach the public were not the problem; rather, it was Johnson's inability to effectively harness the media that led to his downfall. If Johnson's behavior had been more appropriate, his presidency would have represented a natural step in the development of the institution. The increased frequency of popular communication during the Johnson administration was an attempt to navigate a complicated media environment and reach the public directly. Even though Johnson was unsuccessful, many of his successors used similar strategies, including extensive touring and interviews with newspaper correspondents, leading to a general trend of increased speaking frequency.

Interlude: Ulysses S. Grant (1869–1877)

After Johnson's tumultuous presidency, the American people were eager for a break from the "bloodshed and partisan wrangling" (Tebbel and Watts 1985, 216). In this spirit, General Ulysses S. Grant was elected president in 1868 as a Civil War hero with a "huge storehouse of goodwill" (Calhoun 2010, 30). He received 300,000 more votes than his opponent. The newly enfranchised African Americans cast an estimated 500,000 votes for Grant, representing a potentially important new voting bloc for Republicans (Calhoun 2010, 16). In a nod to this new constituency, President Grant addressed violence at the polls in his annual message (Calhoun 2010, 30).

While Grant himself remained mostly unscathed, his administration was plagued with corruption. This corruption pushed the media to begin the practice of investigating the president and his administration, setting up an adversarial relationship. The problems began with Grant's cabinet appointments, many of whom were family members and were seen as unfit. For the most part, though, Grant fulfilled the ceremonial role the public envisioned for him. Following in Johnson's footsteps, Grant occasionally gave interviews to the *New York Herald*'s Washington correspondent, G. De. B. Keim (Tebbel and Watts 1985, 219).

Scholars cite a number of explanations for Grant's minimal interaction with the public. First, because of Grant's background as a military man, not a politician, he had little understanding of or need for the press (Pollard 1947). Second, Grant made a deal with the Radical Republicans, which led to his subservience to Congress (Laracey 2002). Third, as a former Union general, Grant was still "reviled by whites in the former Confederacy," so he had little to gain from touring those states (Frantz 2011, 28). Last, although he was a great leader, Grant was a weak public speaker and preferred to be a "unifying figure who stayed above the passions of politics" (Ellis 2008, 99). In sum, Grant had little to gain by pursuing new public communication opportunities. Instead, he was constrained by circumstances.

Rutherford B. Hayes (1877–1881)

Rutherford B. Hayes was responsible for the next significant increase in spoken popular presidential communication. He used public rhetoric to establish his legitimacy after an especially contentious electoral process and to stake out a position on civil service reform separate from that of his party (Pluta 2021).[11] Hayes made more speeches per year than any previous president, and he had a clear legislative agenda, consistently promoting the same five items: no second term, civil service reform, specie payments, universal education, and equal rights (Calhoun 2010). Hayes mentioned these issues in his nomination acceptance letter, his inaugural address, his annual messages, and on tour.

Hayes made it clear that he cared about public opinion and the judgment of the people. After issuing a special message on the silver bill in March 1878, Hayes wrote, "I am not liked as a president by the politicians in office, in the press, or in Congress. But I am content to abide by the judgement—the sober second thought—of the people" (Hayes 1922, 463). He also wrote about the popular reception of his annual message and veto message, confirming that these were intended not only for Congress but also for the American public.

The most difficult issue Hayes faced during his presidency was civil service reform, because his position put him at odds with some of his fellow Republicans in Congress. In an interview with the *New York Times* recapping the president's accomplishments, a representative of the administration said, "Whatever President Hayes has done or failed to do in establishing a system of civil service reform, he has at least kept the subject very thoroughly before the people. He knows as well as anybody how little notice Congress takes of the President's Message; but he knows also the public can be educated by the persistent talking over the heads of their representatives" ("Hayes Administration," March 2, 1881, 1). This insight indicates that presidents in this period had little ability to directly influence Congress, but it also illustrates an early example of "going public." Whether Hayes's efforts were successful is hard to judge, since he stayed true to his promise not to run for reelection. However, he set a precedent that a number of his successors, including Benjamin Harrison and William McKinley, not only followed but also expanded.

Data and Methods

My data for Hayes include 234 pieces of spoken popular communication. In addition, I used his nomination acceptance letter, his inaugural address, four annual messages, and twelve veto messages (available online from the American Presidency Project). I also used biographies of Hayes; histories of the period 1877–1881; historical newspaper accounts of the Hayes administration and its communication strategies, including coverage of the inauguration, annual messages, vetoes, tours, and other speeches; and other primary source documents, including the president's diary. In these communications, Hayes repeatedly addressed his legitimacy and that of the federal government, called for national unity, advanced his legislative agenda, and even campaigned for others (unusual for nineteenth-century presidents).

Nomination Acceptance Letter and Inaugural Address

By 1876, it was customary for presidential candidates to state their policy positions in a letter when accepting the party's nomination. Though technically not part of the corpus of presidential rhetoric, the acceptance letter had become "a central campaign document in which candidates were expected to layout their views on the important issues" (Ellis 1998, 115), and it represents a natural starting point for this analysis. Hayes's letter focused on five items: civil service reform, no second term, subsidized public education, resumption of specie payments, and a government in the South that respected the rights of all citizens (Hoogenboom 1995). These issues can be viewed as Hayes's policy platform, and much like twentieth- and twenty-first-century presidents, he addressed these issues consistently while in office, beginning with his inaugural address delivered on March 5, 1877. Hayes's inaugural message was intended for a popular audience, and it called for national unity, addressed the legitimacy of his election, and laid out his policy platform. The new president adhered to many of the same themes as his predecessors and highlighted the enduring bond between the president and the public. Like almost three-quarters of presidents, Hayes asked for the American people's help in governing (Ericson 1997).

The first half of the address focused on the aftermath of the Civil War and Reconstruction. Hayes tried to encourage unity and forgiveness while at the same time asking the country to consider the plight of the newly freed African Americans. References to important events, such as the Civil War, can be viewed as "significant legitimizing elements of contested presidencies" (Abbott, Thompson, and Sarbaugh-Thompson 2002, 210).

Again like almost 75 percent of other presidents, Hayes laid out his general policy proposals, including adherence to the new constitutional amendments, universal education, and the resumption of specie payments. In the case of specie payments, Hayes advocated for legislation in Congress and mentioned public support for the issue. In invoking the theme of popular support, Hayes and other presidents "willingly place themselves within a democratic culture" (Ericson 1997, 740). Press analysis of the inaugural address noted that similar issues had been covered in the nomination acceptance letter ("Mr. Hayes Inaugural Address," *New York Times*, March 6, 1877, 4). The *New York Times* commonly published public reaction to important presidential speeches from papers around the country. Excerpts from southern papers show that many in the South were skeptical of Hayes's ability to follow through on his promise to end Reconstruction ("The Inaugural Address: How It Is Received and Commented on by the Southern Press," *New York Times*, March 9, 1877, 8).

In his inaugural address, Hayes directly confronted the circumstances of his election. He praised the tribunal chosen to determine the outcome of the election, noting that the committee was "entitled to [the] fullest confidence of the American people." The president also mentioned that the decision had been accepted as "legally conclusive by the general judgement of the public." As I will show, Hayes's efforts to establish the legitimacy of his administration were often centered on public support, making his popular communication a central aspect of his presidency.

Messages to Congress

The final act in establishing a successful succession is "presiding over a major government function," which for most modern US presidents is a speech to a joint session of Congress (Abbott et al. 2002, 209). However, in the late 1800s there was a significant interval between the president's inauguration in March and his first message to Congress in December. Hayes filled this void by touring extensively in his first year to shore up his legitimacy (discussed in detail in the next section).

Despite the timing, the annual message remained an important part of popular presidential communication in the nineteenth century. Hayes began to work on his first annual message in October 1877, writing in his diary that he must start preparing the message and would look to his predecessors for the proper format (Hayes 1922). On December 3, 1877,

Hayes delivered his first annual message to Congress, stating that to solidify his legitimacy, the president should present himself as a "combination of national booster and competent manager whose skill and knowledge inspire the confidence of the public and political elites" (Abbott et
al. 2002, 209). Hayes did that by addressing the important issues facing
the country. He discussed sectional unity and how the administration's
policies had encouraged reconciliation; stressed the importance of legislation to resume specie payments; continued his campaign for civil service reform; and gave a rundown of the state of the economy and commerce, a standard topic for these messages.

Hayes knew that some Republicans opposed him, in part because of
his attempts to reform the civil service and reduce patronage. However,
the president believed "a large majority of the best people are in full ac-
cord with me" (Hayes 1922, 449), and he pressed forward with his reform
agenda, using his annual messages as powerful public relations tools
(Paul 1998). Significantly, "Hayes' argument was founded in his reading
of public opinion, rather than in timeless, 'universal' values—as previous
presidents were wont to do" (Paul 1998, 71). His numerous successes on
this issue "gave the president a taste of the political benefits to be obtained
by stirring public passions in other areas" (Paul 1998, 74).

Beyond establishing legitimacy, annual messages were the president's
best opportunity to promote his legislative agenda. Hayes stuck closely to
his policy platform in each of his annual messages. Civil service reform
was mentioned in all but the third annual message; the resumption of
specie payments and the importance of subsidized public education were
mentioned in each annual message; and civil rights was mentioned in all
but the third annual message.

Hayes's strategic use of the annual message illustrates its importance
to nineteenth-century presidents for conveying their policy positions to
the public, despite being a written document. The annual message was
published in all major (and many minor) newspapers around the country. Typically, newspapers printed a preview of the message a few days
before it was delivered to Congress, the text of the message on the day

after it was delivered, and commentary for a week or so thereafter. Regardless of whether these messages were spoken by the president in front of Congress, they were intended to present the president's policies to the people. Practically speaking, printing these messages in newspapers was by far the best way for nineteenth-century presidents, including Hayes, to reach the public (Cornwell 1979).

The language in the headlines illustrates that newspaper publishers and readers viewed the annual message as a way for the president to communicate his policy views to the public. Headlines such as "Hayes on Specie" and "Hayes Financial Policy" (*Chicago Daily Tribune*, December 5, 1877, 2) indicate a clear intention to link the message with the president, his policy objectives, and his views.

Another indication of the importance of the annual message was its increasing length. From 1864 until 1910, the length of the message grew steadily. This growth and the greater focus on issues and positions could be understood as a product of the president's "awareness that the public held the keys to the White House" and a reflection of the president's closer relationship with Congress and the public (Teten 2003, 341). Hayes's messages averaged 10,896 words, almost 1,800 more words than Grant and 600 more than Arthur.

Tours

Despite the importance of the annual message, Hayes did most of his public communicating on tour—setting the stage for future presidents to do the same. Hayes leveraged the railroad and his speaking ability on the stump to his advantage, traveling across the country and reaching tens of thousands of Americans. While on tour, Hayes addressed the general public as well as groups with specific interests, including newly freed and enfranchised African Americans, veterans, and business organizations (Pluta 2014).

Sectional reconciliation was one of the president's goals and a significant impetus for many of his tours. Though dismissed by some contemporary scholars, regional sectionalism was a significant political issue in the late nineteenth century (Frantz 2011; Deacon 2011). But before going south, Hayes first headed north to shore up his base of support there, speaking frequently about the importance of national unity (Hayes 1922, 424). After returning from his first two tours, Hayes wrote in his diary that "the people seemed pleased" and that he had "tried to impress the people with the importance of harmony between different Sections, States, classes, and races, and to discourage sectionalism and race and class prejudice" (Hayes 1922, 443). He also commented on his upcoming trip to the South and the importance of encouraging unity in that part of the country.

In the fall of his first year in office, Hayes set out on a tour of the South to promote national unity after the pain of the Civil War and Reconstruction (Edwards 1878; Morgan 1969, 23; Hoogenboom 1995; Calhoun 2006; Deacon 2011). Charles W. Calhoun called the northern and southern tours a "public relations blitz" for Hayes's reconciliation policies (2006, 147). Hayes frequently reminded southerners about their "promise to observe the Amendments" (Simpson 1998, 213; Frantz 2002). Much like Millard Fillmore before him, Hayes not only called for unity in his rhetoric but also illustrated it in the makeup of his traveling party, which included his cabinet and prominent southerners such as Wade Hampton (De Santis 1955; Slagell 2008). Many scholars argued that the tour was "modern" because Hayes assessed the success of his southern policy of pacification (De Santis 1955; Davison 1972; Trefousse 2002; Slagell 2008).

Hayes's tour of the South (September 1877) was covered in detail not only in the daily newspapers but also in a pamphlet published in 1878 and titled *The President's Tour South. A Triumphal March through the "Solid South." Enthusiastic Reception of the President and Cabinet at All Points along the Journey. Speeches, Sayings and Doings of Those Who Participated in the Ovation to the President.* It attempted to include every utterance the president made on the trip. The pamphlet's introduction explained the political circumstances, specifically the Civil War and Reconstruction, and concluded that President Hayes's election signaled an end to sectional bitterness. In summarizing the trip, the editor noted the importance of the railroad to the group's ability to cover vast ground. In addition to his cabinet, Hayes was accompanied by twenty-five "historians of the journey."

The *President's Tour South* pamphlet included a biography of each member of Hayes's cabinet, indicating the importance of the administration's political platform. For example, it noted that George W. McCray, the secretary of war, "has been one of the most prominent advocates of a thorough and radical reform of the Civil Service." After his first three tours, Hayes assessed his presidency, concluding that so far it had been "successful" and that "the good people approv[ed] of what I am trying to do" (Hayes 1922, 473).

In the run-up to the 1878 midterm elections, Hayes embarked on a tour of the Midwest (Wisconsin, Minnesota, Illinois, Ohio, and Pennsylvania), "arguing that a sound currency was indispensable to prosperity" (Calhoun 2010, 61). In addition to being a key aspect of his legislative agenda, Hayes "believed a unified GOP based on the money question could eclipse internal divisions" and be beneficial to the party's electoral prospects (Calhoun 2010, 61). The president reassured the people that his administration's economic policy would continue to benefit the country and that the purpose of this tour was to "convince inflation-minded midwesterners—among whom the 'spread of the Greenback heresy' was 'appalling'—that the resumption of specie payments in January 1879 would strengthen the economy" (Hoogenboom 1995, 372).

Hayes gave the tour's keystone speech at the Minnesota State Fair. In it, the president "set forth in detail the great reduction in the national debt, with the consequent diminution of the annual interest charge, the decrease in public expenditures and the lowering of taxes, and the vast increase in foreign trade, the exports for the current year being the largest in the history of the country" (Williams 1914, 257).

Hayes's tour of the central West in September 1879 began with a speech at the annual reunion of his old regiment at Youngstown, Ohio.

This very long speech was "so clear and forceful an exposition of Mr. Hayes's conception of the fundamental principles of our dual system of government, of the causes and results of the Civil War, of the duty of maintaining unimpaired the settlements of the war in favor of equal rights and the supremacy of the laws of the nation," that the entire speech was reprinted in Charles Richard Williams's biography of Hayes (Williams 1914, 269). Williams wrote, "this speech attracted universal attention and for days was the most important topic of editorial discussion" (1914, 276). Democratic papers were quick to condemn the president for "making a political speech on such an occasion" and for abandoning "his policy of conciliation" (Williams 1914, 276). The language of this speech mirrored Hayes's letter of acceptance, inaugural address, and rhetoric on his southern tour (Williams 1914, 276; Trefousse 2002). The following day at Detroit, Hayes gave a speech that focused on public debt and the administration's efforts to reduce it and encourage economic growth. Hayes continued his travels through the Midwest, repeating the substantive points of these two speeches (Williams 1914, 281; Trefousse 2002, 116). My own examination of Hayes's rhetoric finds that he consistently addressed the core issues established in his nomination acceptance letter.

The president's western tour in 1880 also had national and sectional unity as a goal (Baur 1955; Deacon 2011). Although the southern states' position gets more attention, "during the civil war, the western states' and territories' alliance to the federal government had been shaky at best" (Deacon 2011, 170). Not surprisingly, with only months left in his term, Hayes was more "informal and familiar" than on previous trips (Williams 1914, 294; Davison 1972). Despite the ceremonial content, this tour "was a further advancement of American unity" (Baur 1955, 33).

Hayes claimed all his tours were nonpolitical, but observers agree that he rarely did anything that was apolitical and that his southern tour in particular had "high political importance" (Frantz 2011, 23; Hoogenboom 1995). It is important to note that nineteenth-century presidents often used "nonpolitical" to mean "nonpartisan." This distinction was especially important to Hayes, who was an advocate of civil service reform to eliminate patronage. The difference between political and partisan might include avoiding criticism of opponents but still "contributing effectively to the Republican cause by helping to dissipate men's fears of the effect of resumption of specie payments and by quickening their hopes of better times" (Williams 1914, 267). Hayes defended the policies of his administration and made a case for their continuation but avoided explicit criticism of his political opponents (Ellis 2008).

Contemporary newspaper opinion was split on whether the southern tour, in particular, was political. In the South, editors had a political agenda and a real stake in making Hayes's tour seem illegitimate or meaningless (Frantz 2002). Northern editorial opinion was divided on the nature of the president's tour. On the one hand, Hayes was putting himself above party and section; on the other hand, the tour's positive results would benefit the Republicans in future elections, making the tour inherently political in the opinion of some editors (Frantz 2002, 67). The amount of newspaper coverage and editorials devoted to Hayes's tour provided evidence of its contemporary relevance and importance.

Going on tour, especially to the South, involved political risk. This led Hayes to be cautious in "his public utterances and in his correspondence . . . lest they be distorted or otherwise misused by a careless or hostile press" (Pollard 1947, 457). Andrew Johnson's swing around the country almost ten years earlier had taught politicians this lesson.

As I have shown, a significant portion of Hayes's spoken rhetoric took place on tour. This illustrates two important aspects of the evolution of popular presidential communication. The first is the importance of technological innovation. Before radio, touring was the only way for a president's speeches to reach a significant part of the public. And of course, the way to reach the greatest number of Americans was through the newspaper. The second is the importance of the railroad to the president's ability to travel, especially as the country grew. The larger point is that, given the significant variation in how much presidents spoke to the public during this time, factors beyond technology were in play.

Interviews

Much like Johnson before him, Hayes gave interviews to newspaper correspondents. Most major newspapers, including the *New York Times*, *Washington Post*, and *San Francisco Chronicle*, published these interviews. Significantly, a majority of these interviews took place in the first year of the president's term, as Hayes worked to overcome the fallout from a contentious and controversial election. Table 3.4 lists the interviews given by Hayes and the topics covered. These interviews were an important step in the evolution of popular presidential communication, as they represented another effort by presidents to reach the people directly and navigate an increasingly complex media environment.

Understanding the Exceptions: Chester Arthur (1881–1885) and Grover Cleveland (1885–1889)

As figure 3.1 illustrates, the trend toward greater speech making was not universal to late nineteenth-century presidents. Chester Arthur (forty-nine speeches) and Grover Cleveland (fifty-three speeches in his first term) were both comparatively quiet, despite having the same access to the railroad as Johnson, Hayes, and Harrison. Much as Grant had little to gain from communicating with the public, Arthur and Cleveland had their own reasons for limiting the amount of spoken public rhetoric in which they engaged.

Arthur became president when James Garfield was assassinated early in his term (shot on July 2, 1881, and died on September 19). As an accidental president, Arthur was already at a disadvantage. However, his situation was made worse because he disliked living at the White House and being president. More importantly, he had Bright's disease, a chronic kidney condition that often left him tired and weak. Arthur had no interest in having a relationship with the press and shut them out completely. The public had become accustomed to hearing regularly from the chief executive, so Arthur's silence was detrimental to his goals. The press had

Table 3.4: Rutherford B. Hayes Interviews[a]

Date	Headline	Newspaper	Interviewer	Topic
March 10, 1877	Hayes Southern Policy President	Chicago Tribune	Senator Conover (R-FL)	Southern policy
April 15, 1877	Hayes Accords an Interview to a Press Reporter	New York Times	Newspaperman	Southern policy
May 10, 1877	A Short Political Chat with the President	San Francisco Chronicle	Newspaperman	Southern policy
June 12, 1877	President Hayes on Silver	New York Times	Governor Cullum (R-IL)	Silver
September 11, 1877	President Hayes and the South	New York Times	Newspaperman	Southern policy
January 12, 1879	Interview with a Newspaper Man	Chicago Tribune	Newspaperman	Sectional unity
September 15, 1879	Interview in Cincinnati	Chicago Tribune	Newspaperman	Sectional unity
November 1, 1879	To the Editor of the Intelligencer	New York Times	Newspaperman	Sectional unity
December 9, 1879	To the Representative of the Boston Herald	New York Times	Newspaperman	Currency
March 26, 1880	Interview with a Correspondent of the Tribune	Chicago Tribune	Newspaperman	Currency
August 14, 1880	Interview in Pittsburg	Chicago Tribune	Newspaperman	Sectional unity

[a]This list of interviews is provided in Pollard (1947, 414). I have all these interviews in my data set, although some might be republished versions (if the original newspaper has not been digitized).

little choice but to interpret the president's behavior as they saw fit (Pollard 1947). The politics of the time also limited Arthur. The Democrats controlled both houses of Congress and Arthur had alienated his own party, leaving him essentially alone (Laracey 2002, 127).[12]

Grover Cleveland, the lone Democrat elected in a Republican era, demonstrated the utility of written rhetoric for pre-radio presidents.[13] Cleveland, like his hero Jackson, saw himself as the only "official elected by all the people, one whose principal function was to defend them from corrupt interests" (Calhoun 2010, 98). In this capacity, Cleveland vetoed almost four hundred bills, twice the number of his predecessors combined. Cleveland also appealed to the public in his annual messages, special messages, and veto messages (Laracey 2002; Hoffman 2010, 60).

Like many pre–Civil War presidents, Cleveland communicated with the public through writings rather than speeches (Hoffman 2002). Cleveland's preference for written communication was both political and practical. This strategy allowed him to reach a large swath of the public and to avoid speaking, which became especially important after he had oral surgery to remove a tumor.

To ensure the passage of tariff legislation, Cleveland devoted his entire third annual message (December 6, 1887) to the topic (Calhoun 2010). The *New York Times* called the message a "startling novelty." Editor, essayist, journalist, and novelist George William Curtis noted:

> It is a document addressed rather to what Mr. Lincoln used to "call the plain people of the country" rather than Congress alone. He undoubtedly intended that the message should be just what it was called—an elementary treatise. It furnishes everyman who is busy with his work day both arguments and answers around the central question it discusses. In this way it tends to make a strong public opinion for the policy which the President advocates. ("The President's Problem," *New York Times*, December 10, 1887, 5)

It is worth noting that Curtis explicitly saw the message as directed at both the public and Congress—as was the case for most of the nineteenth century.

Benjamin Harrison (1889–1893)

Like fellow Republican Rutherford B. Hayes, Benjamin Harrison spoke frequently to the public, taking a number of tours during his four years in office. In addition, Harrison was intimately involved in the legislative process, cajoling members of Congress and communicating with the public regularly in both speech and writing. Through his leadership, the Fifty-First Congress was one of the most productive up to that time (Calhoun 2010, 125). Despite midterm losses, Republicans could look back at the Fifty-First Congress as one of remarkable accomplishment: they passed 531 public laws. Harrison played a key role in the legislative process, employing both public pronouncements and behind-the-scenes lobbying and negotiation (Calhoun 2010). His actions would provide important lessons for presidents to come.

Harrison used written rhetoric to express his views on important issues. In a letter to Colonel R. E. Thomas of Mechanicsburg, secretary and general manager of the National Granger's Exhibition, Harrison wrote in July 1890 that he hoped to appear at the event because "this tariff question which is now before the people is the most important question of the day and the people should be formally educated on it." The president continued, "This free trade question is a dangerous one to handle and if it should win in 1892 it would cause great distress throughout the land, something never experienced by the American people" (*New York Times*, July 12, 1890, 1). The publishing of seemingly private correspondence between the president and various individuals or organizations was commonplace in the nineteenth century.[14]

The run-up to the 1890 midterm elections included a backlash against the historically productive legislative session of the Fifty-First Congress. The McKinley Tariff Act (1890) was seen as particularly damaging. President Harrison embarked on a speaking tour through the Midwest in October, attempting to defend against the insurgent Farmers' Alliance and warning farmers not to fall for "unsafe expedients" (Calhoun 2010, 131). Harrison toured for a week (October 6–13) and gave forty-two speeches on topics such as national unity, education, and economic prosperity. His persistent theme of prosperity was in fact a clear reference to the success of Republican tariff policies (Korzi 2004, 175; Calhoun 2006, 108). Unfortunately, the tour failed to prevent massive GOP losses in November.

With Congress in the hands of the Democrats, Harrison was unable to accomplish much in his last two years in office. However, he continued to engage vigorously with the American public, encouraging the evolution of popular presidential communication. According to my data, Harrison gave at least 200 speeches after the midterm losses, including at least 138 speeches during a thirty-one-day tour in the spring of 1891 (April 14– May 15), which some scholars consider the first national tour by a president (Frantz 2011).[15] On this tour, Harrison addressed economic diversification, reunion, and the supremacy of law, as he traveled through parts of the South, West, and Midwest.

A number of things had changed since Hayes's 1877 tour. The country now included six new western states. By this time, the Republican Party had mostly abandoned the project of Reconstruction and was instead presenting a conciliatory approach to the South. On tour, "when Harrison argued about the importance of adhering to the Constitution, or raised specific policy issues such as tariffs, he was appealing not to any particular region but to the entire country" (Frantz 2011, 57). In commentary about the tour, the *New York Times* noted, "Mr. Harrison, whose policy in office has been of a very narrow sort, who has been a very persistent and bigoted partisan in almost all directions, and whose partisanship has often taken an offensive sectional turn, has found himself able and willing, perhaps even forced to assume a tone of pretty broad national patriotism, and logically to discredit a great deal that he had before expressed" ("Mr. Harrison's Tour," May 4, 1891, 4). This comment clarifies a point of confusion for some scholars. Although speeches given on tours may seem to be simply platitudes and general statements without policy content, contemporary observers gleaned much more meaning from these speeches. As the Republicans moved away from Reconstruction, they embraced less "partisan" speech—which may appear ceremonial out of context. See table 3.1 for a summary of Harrison's tours.

Even in the post–Civil War period, when the frequency of spoken rhetoric increased dramatically, written public communication by presidents was considered important because there was no other way to reach the public as a whole. The *New York Times* analyzed a letter from Harrison to the Western States Commercial Commerce in Kansas City:

> Not less striking than his speeches, and rising to the dignity of a special message to the country, is the president's letter to the Kansas City Congress. This is a serious and weighty discussion of the questions that are first in the public estimation on the West. If such speeches and letters as these endeavoring to present issues fairly, in condensed form, omitted nothing essential, are incident to systematic seeking of the public favor, they must be classified as extraordinarily handsome electioneering and worthy the close attention of the whole people. ("Mr. Harrison's Extra Message," April 15, 1891, 4)

Clearly, this contemporary commentary indicates that written rhetoric and spoken rhetoric were considered identical as statements of the president's policy preferences.

Conclusion

Unsurprisingly, the roots of going public can be found in this era. The railroad provided presidents with their first opportunity to address citizens who might disagree with them, which had been largely impossible in the partisan newspaper era. This strategy had its shortfalls, as Andrew Johnson's tour illustrated, but as the railroad expanded and travel became easier, presidents utilized these opportunities more often. Additionally, as the nineteenth century wore on, the persuadable public grew because party strength ebbed, the Republicans made overtures to southerners, and the country faced new problems. These factors combined to increase the incentives for presidents to speak with the public and attempt to influence public opinion.

In the period between the Civil War and the invention of the radio, presidents turned to speech more often, but written rhetoric continued to be an essential element of their communication strategies. Written communication became a secondary form of communication in the twentieth century as technology facilitated more frequent speech. In the twenty-first century, the rise of the internet and social media encouraged the return of written communication with the public to some extent, but as the next chapter shows, there has been a steady trend toward greater communication overall.

4

Going Almost National: Grover Cleveland to
Woodrow Wilson, 1894–1921

At the turn of the twentieth century, a number of factors combined to push presidents closer to having a truly national audience. Political parties weakened further, the press professionalized, and innovations in communication technologies continued. The makeup of the electorate was also changing, with the emergence of the first mass-market consumer economy and the growth of a middle class (Arnold 2009, 11). This new middle class took on new importance in politics as working-class voters became less interested in politics—79.3 percent of eligible voters turned out 1896, but that dropped to 65.2 percent by 1904 (Arnold 2009, 11).

Parties were weakened by progressive reformers, economic depression, and perceived corruption (Ryfe 2005). At the same time, economic conditions and new norms of professionalization led to the growth of an independent press (Schudson 2001; Ryfe 2005). By 1900, more than 85 percent of daily newspapers in the fifty largest US cities were nonpartisan (Hamilton 2006, 53). In concert, these two trends had consequences for presidential rhetoric. The new independent newspapers "informed citizens, and they also provided a means for broadcasting, so to speak, the president's message in [a] way that was not immediately dependent on his political party" (Arnold 2009, 11).

Relatedly, "the decline of parties and electoral competition in the early twentieth century" gave interest groups an opportunity to influence policy (Arnold 2009, 12). The growth of interest groups had direct ramifications for presidential rhetoric as presidents addressed these groups much more often. Together, these forces caused presidential rhetorical strategies to become more "national," although the final steps in this process would not occur until the widespread use of the radio in the 1920s and 1930s.

As many of their predecessors had done, William McKinley, Theodore Roosevelt, and William Howard Taft traveled widely and addressed local crowds. However, these presidents were now likely to emphasize issues of national importance such as the Spanish-American War and the tariff (Pluta 2014). Similarly, Woodrow Wilson led the country through World War I and toured in an effort to gain support for the ill-fated Paris peace treaty, another issue of national importance.

Although these presidents were well traveled and their speeches were often reprinted in newspapers, their ability to shape public opinion was still limited because it was dependent on engagement by the public, whether that meant attending a presidential speech in person or reading the newspaper. This prevented presidents in this period from having a truly national audience that experienced their messages simultaneously, as distinguished from the next era, when the radio revolutionized the president's ability to reach the American public.

The Content of Popular Presidential Communication

The frequency of spoken popular presidential communication had been steadily increasing for decades. In response to some of the same forces, the content of these speeches was changing as well. While strong parties limited the need for some presidents to explicitly set an agenda in the pre–Civil War era, in the later part of the nineteenth century presidents increasingly advocated for specific legislation (Korzi 2004). Some consider Wilson's presidency a watershed in the mode of presidential communication, but by then, presidents had been addressing more of their rhetoric to the public for decades (Pluta 2015). In accordance with a growing and democratizing audience, the content of presidential rhetoric was simplifying (Lim 2008; Pluta 2015). Whether this was normatively bad for democracy is a subject of scholarly debate that I address briefly. The media environment and technological change made it more attractive for presidents to pursue persuasion as they were able to reach larger portions of the public.

Grover Cleveland (1893–1897) and the Tariff

As discussed in the previous chapter, Grover Cleveland, the only Democrat elected in a predominantly Republican age, used spoken rhetoric less frequently than many of his contemporaries.[1] However, Cleveland used other communication strategies in an effort to influence tariff legislation, including devoting his third annual message (1887, during his first term) to that topic (Hoffman 2002; Calhoun 2010). He continued to work to pass tariff legislation in his second, nonconsecutive term (1893–1897). These efforts would be instructive for Wilson two decades later.

Cleveland sent a letter to the chairman of the House Ways and Means Committee in the summer of 1894. This letter was also released to the public in an attempt to move the tariff debate forward. Efforts to implement tariff reform had led to confusion and deadlock, and Cleveland's letter was seen as a final push to pass the necessary legislation (Nevins 1962). To Cleveland, tariff reform legislation would fulfill a promise to the public, and he stated, "I have so often promised its realization to my fellow-countrymen as a result of their trust and confidence in the Democratic Party" ("The Fight Is On," *Washington Post*, July 20, 1894, 1).

Though there was little reaction to Cleveland's letter in the House, the Senate responded passionately, and one of the president's opponents charged that Cleveland was violating "the spirit of the Constitution" (Nevins 1962, 582). There are a few things to note here: The president was not speaking to the public about policy in this case; he had sent a letter to a committee chair. Thus, he was not violating any norm prohibiting presidents from engaging in policy talk with the public. Political opponents regularly and eagerly invoke violation of the Constitution on myriad issues to try to curtail presidential power, acknowledging the strength a president derives from his relationship with the people. A true constitutional violation should spark a reaction not only from opponents with motives to derail the president's efforts but also from fellow partisans, other political elites, and the public.[2] Despite this reaction, Cleveland's letter had the "desired effect in calling forth a burst of remonstrance against the Senate obstructionists, but the time had passed when such a demonstration could do any good" (Nevins 1962, 582).

The reaction in newspapers was not nearly as harsh as that of Cleveland's opponents. The *New York Times* (which was friendly to Democrats during this time) reported on July 26 that this letter was "certainly an innovation" and would "virtually . . . give President Cleveland the privilege of addressing the House of Representatives on a question of legislation." In addition, the *New York Times* called Cleveland's letter "a new sensation, a departure not comparable with any other presidential communication that could be remembered" ("The House Stands by Its Bill," July 20, 1894, 1). Reporting by the *Washington Post* made it clear that this letter was an effort by the president to shape legislation ("The Fight Is On," July 20, 1894, 1). Unfortunately, Cleveland's letter came too late, and the tariff bill was defeated. Instead, the Wilson-Gorman bill became law without his signature. Nevertheless, Cleveland had tried to participate actively and vocally in the legislative process.

Cleveland was more successful in his attempt to repeal the Sherman Silver Act in 1896. He used similar strategies as in the tariff fight: a series of public acts to draw attention to the issue and the release of a public letter that discussed the details (Hoffman 2002, 58). The president's repeated use of these techniques suggests that they were perceived as being at least somewhat effective.

The Progressive Movement and the Growth of Pluralism

The proliferation of interest groups is an often overlooked cause of more frequent presidential rhetoric. In the late nineteenth century, America "was a society of island communities" (Wiebe 1967, xiii). Urbanization and industrialization created many problems that local communities had little ability to fix. The Progressive movement looked for solutions to some of these issues through regulation and organization (Wiebe 1967). As pluralism continued to emerge in the early twentieth century, presidents began to speak to a variety of interest groups.

Presidents since Washington had addressed veterans and military groups on tour, but not until Hayes visited the New York Chamber of Commerce (May 14, 1877) did other kinds of associations receive presidential attention. Harrison visited three chambers of commerce (Cincinnati, August 21, 1889; San Francisco, May 1, 1891; Salt Lake City, May 9, 1891), as well as the Board of Trade in Philadelphia (May 1891), the Mechanics Club (August 12, 1890), and the National Education Association (July 12, 1892). Though Cleveland was relatively reserved, he spoke to the Pan American Medical Conference in September 1893. Beginning with McKinley, the groups grew more diverse. He addressed the American Medical Association (June 2, 1897), the American Bar Association (August 2, 1897), and the National Association of Manufacturing (January 27, 1898), in addition to various chambers of commerce and commercial clubs nationwide. Roosevelt added groups such as the Hungarian Republican Club (February 14, 1905), the American Tract Society (March 12, 1905),[3] the National Congress of Mothers (March 13, 1905), and the United Mine Workers (August 10, 1905). Taft spoke to diverse groups, including the National Civic Federation, the Periodical Publisher's Association, and the Catholic Church Jubilee. Sometimes these presidents spoke generally about prosperity and good health, but they often addressed specific policy issues of interest to the group's members. These additions to the president's audience reflected important changes in American democracy.

Going Public: William McKinley (1897–1901)
and Theodore Roosevelt (1901–1909)

McKinley and Roosevelt toured extensively in support of both specific policies and candidates (table 4.1). It was during this time that newspapers began to mention going public as a presidential device to achieve legislative goals, although hints of this strategy had been present during the Hayes, Harrison, and Cleveland administrations. In a speech at Wadena, Minnesota, on October 13, 1899, McKinley presented the issue of the Philippines and claimed that it was in the hands of the people. The president said, "And so all policies and all purposes of President or Congress must finally be submitted to the people, and their judgment when constitutionally rendered is the law of the land."

In the spring of 1898 the United States entered the Spanish-American War, providing McKinley an opportunity to lead the country in wartime on the world stage. The White House press organization had grown over the last fifty years, and McKinley's secretary gave reporters advance copies of his speeches and sent a "steady stream of bulletins" to the wire services (Gould 1982, 101). Lewis Gould makes an important point that is easy to overlook when characterizing McKinley's speeches on tour: "outside the precise political context of October 1898, the speeches seem stuffed with generalities. When read in tandem with the epochal events of the critical year, they become masterful examples of how an adroit leader can set the terms of public discussion in his own favor" (1982, 104). Like Harrison's before him, McKinley's speeches may seem ceremonial when read out of context, but at the time, the public clearly understood the president's positions.

As a congressman, McKinley had "watched Benjamin Harrison's judicious lobbying of Congress, his use of the press, and his willingness to travel and take the case for his policies to the people" (Calhoun 2010, 180). Building on Harrison's successes, McKinley used "his direct appeals to the public to build a power base independent of his constitutionally defined relationship with Congress" (Calhoun 2010, 180). Like Hayes and

Table 4.1: Presidential Tours: William McKinley (1897–1901) and Theodore Roosevelt (1901–1909)

President (Party)/Dates	States Visited	Number of Days	Number of Speeches	Themes
McKinley (R)				
October 14–22, 1898	IA, IL, OH	9	57	Expansion, economic prosperity
December 14–19, 1898	GA, AL	5	10	Sectionalism, economic prosperity
October 6–18, 1899	OH, IL, IN, MN, ND, MI, WI, IA, SD	13	71	Spanish-American War, gold
April 29–May 29, 1901[a]	LA, VA, AL, TN, MS, GA, TX, AZ[b], CA	32	30	Trusts, trade reciprocity, unity
Roosevelt (R)				
April 7–11, 1902	VA, SC	5	12	Economic potential of South
August 22–September 2, 1902	RI, MA	12	46	Trusts
September 6–October 10, 1902	OH, WV, SC, NC	5	14	Trusts, national unity
October 19–24, 1902[c]	PA, OH, MI, WI, MN, IA, NE, IL, MO, KS	6	10	Economy, trusts, army and navy
March 31–June 5, 1904	CA, OR, ID, WI, MN, ND, MT, MO, WA, AZ[b], CO, NM[b], NV, PA	66	263[d]	Monroe Doctrine, tariff, conservation, trusts
April 4–May 10, 1905[e]	KY, TX, PA, OH, OK, CO, NE, IL, IA	38	51	Railroads, citizenship, Panama
October 18–31, 1905	VA, NC, SC, GA, TN, FL, AL, MS, AK, AR, LA	13	36	Railroads, nationalization of life insurance, third term

---

[a]Mrs. McKinley became ill, and for a number of days the president did "not leave her bedside" (*New York Times*, June 4, 1901, 1). The train went directly from San Francisco to Washington, making only a few briefs stops, because of her illness.

[b]Territories at the time of the president's visit.

[c]Roosevelt returned on October 24 because of an abscess on his leg that developed after a trolley accident (*Washington Post*, September 25, 1902, 1).

[d]*Chicago Tribune*, June 19, 1904.

[e]Roosevelt went hunting from April 8 to May 6 and did not give any speeches during this time.

Harrison, McKinley's skill as an orator encouraged this approach (Gould 1982).

When Theodore Roosevelt went on tour in 1905, the *Washington Post* noted, "This is not the first time that President Roosevelt has 'gone to the people' for support against Republican opposition in Congress" ("Appealing to the People," February 11, 1905, 1). The *Post* went on to explain that the practice could be traced to McKinley: "While President Roosevelt's manner of going to the people is more strenuous than was that of any of his predecessors, it is worth noting that, in fact of his going, he is following the example of President McKinley." The *New York Times* told a similar story about Roosevelt going public, although it failed to credit McKinley as the innovator. The *Times* wrote, "To meet this situation he will appeal to the Nation. Several addresses will be delivered by him in various parts of the country after Congress adjourns for the purpose of getting his side of the case before the people and creating a pressure which will compel the Senate to act" ("Roosevelt on the Stump to Fight the Senate," February 6, 1905, 1). One example was Roosevelt's advocacy for passage of the Hepburn bill, which would allow the federal government to regulate railroad shipping rates (Cornwell 1979).

In the spring of 1903 Roosevelt headed west and made a number of speeches on the Monroe Doctrine, the conservation of natural resources, and the tariff along the way (Gould 1991, 110). Roosevelt believed the federal government should manage conservation, so his approach had serious implications for state governments. The *Chicago Tribune* suggested that the president had undertaken this tour so that "he might get in touch with the people and that he might explain to them face to face, as man to man, the policies, internal and foreign, of his administration" ("The President's Tour," May 19, 1904, D4). The *Tribune* correspondent explained, "It was a speechmaking tour in which the president appealed directly to the people for an endorsement of his own acts and his own views."

The Most Talkative: William Howard Taft (1909–1913)

Despite advocating a constrained interpretation of presidential power, William Taft spoke more per year than any president up to that point. In 1909 Taft spoke at least 311 times, eclipsing Roosevelt's previous high of 281 spoken communications in 1903. In 1911 Taft spoke even more often. Newspapers reported that he gave 350 speeches on his thirty-state tour.[4] Shockingly, Taft's average of 193.5 speeches per year over his four-year term remained the highest until the 1960s, when John F. Kennedy spoke more than 250 times per year.

A few things made it difficult for Taft to be reserved in his spoken communications. The first issue was party politics. Taft faced a Republican Party divided between the "Old Guard" and "insurgents," especially on the most pressing issue of the day: the tariff (Korzi 2004). The second complication was competition from Theodore Roosevelt, who initially endorsed Taft but soon became a critic. Taft was also the first president with access to a car, which made traveling in and around Washington, DC, significantly easier and safer. The House appropriated $12,000 to purchase a car for the president in February 1909 ("House Demands Auto," *Washington Post*, February 3 1909, 4).

Early in his presidency, Taft decided to address the tariff. Roosevelt had avoided the issue because he feared it would cause a rift in the Republican Party between western farmers and eastern manufacturers. As the tariff battle continued through the summer of 1909, newspapers called on the president for leadership. Taft would not allow journalists to quote him, saying that he preferred "personal appeals . . . rather than carrying out a public campaign" ("Taft Takes a Hand," *New York Times,* July 13, 1909, 1). In the end, the Payne-Aldrich tariff bill was passed, but it fell short of what the president had hoped for (Goodwin 2013, 599).

A large part of Taft's rhetoric came on tour. He took two nationwide tours and gave close to five hundred speeches. Taft's extended tour in the West was an effort to promote the new tariff bill in parts of the country that were unhappy with it. As the *New York Times* reported on September 4, 1909, it was in the West that "Mr. Taft must face the problem presented in the record of 17 Republican Representatives and 7 Republican Senators voting against Payne-Aldrich." As leader of the Republican Party, Taft needed to convince westerners that he would work to reduce tariffs. The *New York Times* advised Taft that he could "appeal confidently for support to the Senators" and "to the people who elected them."

Assessing Taft's first year in office, journalist Edward G. Lowry found that the president's weakness stemmed from his reliance on Roosevelt: "Mr. Roosevelt derived his political power and prestige directly from the people; Taft derived his political power and prestige from Mr. Roosevelt" (Lowry 1910, 292). Taft was reluctant to go public because he was afraid he would hurt the party, but by refusing to go public, "he revealed he did not understand Republicans' innovation in public leadership" (Arnold 2009, 115). Despite these reservations, Taft spoke often. His view of the presidency is generally perceived as "whiggish" or weak, so it may seem strange that Taft was the most prolific communicator up to this point in American history. However, the politics of the day made it difficult for him to be silent, and his frequent speech making illustrates how important presidential communication on policy issues had become.

Taft struggled to maintain the same relationship with the press and the public that Roosevelt had enjoyed. Perhaps with this in mind, Roosevelt left the country after Taft's inauguration to give the new president some political space. However, newspapers continued to cover Roosevelt as he traveled in Africa and Europe, and when he returned to the United States in 1910, he went on two tours: one west and one south. As the *New*

York Times reported, both trips were "political in nature" and included many speeches that put pressure on Taft ("Roosevelt's Tours," July 15, 1910, 1).

In 1912 Taft campaigned aggressively for reelection, especially once Roosevelt entered the race for the Republican nomination. In January the president was scheduled to tour Ohio, but a serious cold almost forced him to cancel the trip. However, perhaps realizing the gravity of the situation, Taft fought on. That spring he went from state to state campaigning in the Republican primaries. From January to July 1912, Taft gave almost 150 speeches. Taft won the Republican nomination but lost the general election in a three-way race, which included Roosevelt, to Woodrow Wilson.

An Inflection Point? Woodrow Wilson (1913–1921)

Woodrow Wilson is often seen as a linchpin in the development of the rhetorical presidency, in part for his willingness to appear in person before Congress. Instead, I offer Wilson as a natural culmination of this important period of growth in the relationship between the public and the president.

As discussed in chapter 1, Thomas Jefferson ignored the tradition of delivering the annual message in person and chose to send written messages to Congress. Jefferson's decision was rooted in political pressure, his dislike of confrontation, and his poor speaking ability.[5] In April 1913 Wilson reinstated the custom of in-person delivery with a special message on tariff reform. Wilson's speech is often depicted as a constitutional alteration in the appropriate relationship between the president and the public. The idea that Wilson's conception of the president's role led him to fundamentally change it is essential to many aspects of presidential development and deserves careful consideration.

An underlying assumption of the rhetorical presidency hypothesis is that Wilson represents an inflection point in the simplification of presidential rhetoric (Tulis 1987; Lim 2008). I begin by using quantitative methods to examine this assumption. Previous chapters showed how technology, party unity, and the media environment influenced both the mode and the frequency of presidential speech. Now I examine how these factors affected the content of presidential speech.

Speech Content: Data, Indicators, and Method

To test Wilson's influence across time, I used all annual messages and inaugural addresses from 1789 to 2020. Since these data are readily available, I thought it prudent to include both types of rhetorical acts, given their use since the inception of the presidency. First, I ran a linear regression with the dependent variable as the Flesch Readability Score (0–100), which determines the difficulty of comprehending written material.[6] The regression equation included a dummy variable for the Wilson hypothesis, which was assigned a value of 1 for each year after 1913 and 0 otherwise. Additionally, I included a control variable for inaugural addresses. Since the presidency of Andrew Jackson, inauguration speeches, unlike annual messages, have been unambiguously addressed to the public. I also included a lag of the Flesch score to account for the fact that the content of these speeches may be correlated. Last, I included the number of words in each speech. The equation for this regression is:

$$\text{Flesch}_i = \beta_0 + \beta_1 (\text{LagFlesch})_i + \beta_2 (\text{Words})_i + \beta_3 (\text{Year\_Count})_i + \beta_4 (\text{Tulis})_i + \beta_5 (\text{Inaugural})_i + e_i$$

Second, I used a segmentation function to determine at which point the slope of the regression changed significantly. This type of function fits a regression model with segmented relationships between the response and one or more explanatory variables and provides a break-point estimate (Muggeo 2008).[7] In other words, this function can identify when the trend in simplification of presidential speech accelerated.

Speech Content: Results

First, the expectation for the linear regression was that speeches after Wilson would be simpler (i.e., the coefficient for this variable would be positive and statistically significant). Table 4.2 shows the results of this regression. The Wilson dummy variable was positive but not statistically significant. That is, in the presence of a constant trend toward simpler speech, there was no step-level change that coincided with the Wilson administration. As expected, inaugural addresses were, on average, less complex than annual messages, and the difference was statistically significant.

Second, in the test of whether Wilson was an inflection point, the analysis looked for a slope change rather than a step-level change.[8] The results indicate that the mid-1940s, or during Harry Truman's presidency,

**Table 4.2: Results of Regression Analysis of Annual Messages
and Inaugural Addresses, 1789–2020**

Variable	Coefficient
Intercept	17.44***
	(1.82)
Lag Flesch	0.3603***
	(0.0524)
Words	−0.00004***
	(0.00009)
Year count	0.0916***
	(0.014)
Inaugural	6.95***
	(1.17)
Woodrow Wilson	0.198
	(1.94)
R^2 (goodness of fit)	0.76
Observations	294
BP (test for heteroskedasticity)	0.1298

***$p <<< .001$
Note: Robust standard errors are presented in parentheses.

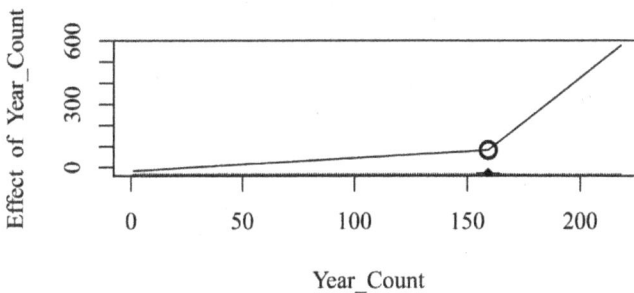

Figure 4.1. Graph of segmentation function indicating when the trend in simplification of presidential speech accelerated. The x-axis shows the variable year_count, which assigns a value of 0 to 1789 and counts up from there. Year_ count 101 is equivalent to 1888. (Source: author's data)

was the most likely place for an acceleration in the pace of simplification (figure 4.1).

As figure 4.1 shows, presidential rhetoric was becoming simpler before 1945, but after that year, the rate of simplification increased. This finding means that prior to 1945, each passing year increased the Flesch score of inaugural addresses and annual messages by 0.05, and after 1945, each additional year increased the Flesch score by 0.175. Both observations are consistent with the idea that presidents are political opportunists, but not with the notion that Wilson shattered a constitutional norm regarding presidential speech. Because of the expansion of radio and TV at this time, it behooved presidents to speak more simply and make their language accessible to a larger audience that was listening to rather than reading most presidential communications. I discuss the effects of radio and TV at length in the next chapter.

The Last Pre-Radio President

The expectation that the president could address the public on matters of public policy, without violating norms, was well established by the time

Wilson took office in 1913. He took the next step, appearing before Congress in person, to gain an advantage in his fight to pass tariff legislation, to claim a political advantage, and to overcome a number of challenges. First, Wilson was elected with a plurality, not a majority, of the popular vote. He won in 1912 because Roosevelt and Taft split the Republican Party vote. Second, the Democrats were not necessarily aligned on the tariff.

Wilson's decision to address Congress in person had a number of advantages. First, by returning to a custom that was more than a hundred years old, Wilson concentrated public attention on his message. This made it less likely that the newspapers would distort or excerpt the message, a practice had been frustrating for earlier presidents (Cornwell 1979, 46). Second, the president focused Congress's full attention on the issue. This strategy was built on Cleveland's use of the annual message in 1887 to narrow public and congressional attention on the tariff issue, at a time when politics had become less central to American life and concerns surrounding industrialization and urbanization took precedence (Calhoun 2010).

Though political scientists often describe Wilson's decision to appear before Congress as rooted in his political philosophy, journalist Oliver P. Newman and Wilson's personal friend Walter Hines Page suggested the idea to the newly elected president as a potential political strategy (Berg 2013; Clements 1992). In an off-the-record interview about executive style on November 6, 1912, Newman suggested that Wilson "might abandon the 112-year old tradition and deliver important speeches in person," and Wilson replied, "Newman that would set them on their ears" (Berg 2013, 292). Page thought that by addressing Congress in person, Wilson could "impress his leadership on the legislature" (Clements 1992, 36).

The media environment in the early twentieth century incentivized Wilson to do whatever he could to capture the public's attention, as politics was losing its preeminent place in the American press. Moreover, the increased professionalization of journalists encouraged the president to reach out to the people directly, circumventing the press as a middle man. The technological constraints of the early 1900s made this very difficult to do on a large scale. However, the desire to cultivate a closer, more direct relationship with the people was not unique to Wilson. Both his predecessors and his successors continually exploited technological advancements to connect more directly with the people (Pluta 2013, 2014).

In-Person Congressional Address: Data and Methods

To gauge the contemporary reaction to Wilson's move, I used data from two newspaper archives: one including only the *Washington Post* and the *New York Times*, and the other consisting of a much larger database. In total, I reviewed 780 articles addressing the event of Wilson's in-person message to Congress.[9] These articles appeared both before and after the president's speech. In addition, I read the *Congressional Record* for April 7, 1913, the day Congress debated Wilson's announcement that he would deliver his special message in person. Last, I consulted biographies of Wilson, including one by Link (2017) and another by Berg (2013).

A search of the *Washington Post* and *New York Times* for the day of Wilson's announcement (April 7) and the day after it (April 8) returned six articles directly related to the issue of the president speaking before Congress; four appeared on the front page. A search of these newspapers for April 9–30 returned eight additional articles directly related to Wilson delivering his special message to Congress in person.

In addition, a search of the Chronicling America database (published by the National Endowment for the Humanities) for the date range April 7–8, 1913 (the first article related to Wilson's speech appeared on the seventh), using the keywords "Wilson, tariff, message, Congress," returned 135 results. Of these 135 articles, 68 appeared on the front page. This database contains many local newspapers, and their articles often drew extensively from those published in other papers such as the *Washington Post* or *New York Times* and shared through the Associated Press. A search of this database over a longer time frame (April 7–30, 1913) returned 770 articles, 326 of which were on the front page. This broader search revealed that local newspapers sometimes took days to publish news stories from the capital. It also allowed me to discover editorial commentary on Wilson's decision and its aftermath.

Of the 326 front-page articles, 30 appeared on April 7, 1913 (table 4.3). These articles had various headlines, but the text largely reprinted one of three articles. The first article, reprinted ten times from the Associated Press, mentioned Adams's and Jefferson's role in delivery of the special message, gave Wilson's reasons for reverting to the old custom, and mentioned Congress members' surprise that the president was going to the Capitol in "the spirit of friendly cooperation" ("The President Will Appear in Person before Congress," *Times Dispatch* [VA], April 7, 1913, 1). This article also acknowledged that some of Wilson's friends were concerned that his in-person appearance might be "fraught with embarrassment." The second article, which appeared in eight different papers, explained the logistics of the president's speech but also mentioned the surprise of members of Congress. The *New York Sun* and the *Washington Herald* printed a slightly different, more supportive article. These newspapers also emphasized the precedent for Wilson's actions, mentioned the constitutional warrant for the president's appearance, and registered excitement (as opposed to concern) on the part of members of Congress. The *Washington Times* focused on the Democratic majority and devoted only a paragraph to Wilson's speech. Finally, newspapers in Hawaii, Oklahoma, Washington, and Oregon reprinted short paragraphs about the tariff and Wilson's decision. Two other articles addressed Wilson and the tariff but not the president's decision to deliver a spoken message.

Forty front-page articles appeared on April 8, 1913 (table 4.4). Sixteen were reprints of one of the articles from April 7. Of the remaining twenty-four, seven were the same article, which described the packed galleries as Wilson arrived on Capitol Hill. Sixteen papers reprinted Wilson's speech in full on the front page. Although there was more variety in the articles published on April 8, the content was reasonably similar. Most articles lauded Wilson's appearance and described a packed House with many dignitaries. An exception was a largely critical article from the *New York Tribune*.

As tables 4.3 and 4.4 illustrate, although coverage was nationwide, there were few competing interpretations of events past or present. This finding was to be expected, as the press had become more professional and less partisan by this time. Since newspapers often shared stories, articles were becoming more descriptive and objective, but they also confirmed that there was no violation of norms.

Thomas Jefferson's Innovation

In an effort to put Wilson's innovation into context, it is useful to revisit the first time the practice of delivering messages to Congress was changed and how that precedent was understood in 1913. The first mention of Wilson's decision to present his tariff message in person appeared on April 7, 1913. Newspapers across the country, including the *Washington Post, New York Times*, and *Wall Street Journal*, reported that the president was reviving the century-old practice of speaking to Congress in person. Journalists reminded readers that both George Washington and John Adams had delivered speeches to Congress and that Thomas Jefferson had abandoned the practice.

In attempting to explain Jefferson's decision to deliver the annual message in writing, 1913 newspaper reports cited the "Lyons Incident."[10] During John Adams's presidency, Representative Matthew Lyon objected to the custom of delivering the annual message as a speech.[11] Lyon refused to participate in the ceremony and procured a promise from Jefferson to refrain from presenting his message as a speech in the future.[12] At the time, as writers recalled in 1913, Federalists criticized Jefferson for this new custom ("Wilson to Read Message in House," *Washington Post*, April 7, 1913, 4). Another *Washington Post* article suggested that partisanship in Congress drove Jefferson to abandon the oral message because the president was afraid "if he ventured to read his message to a Congress

Table 4.3: Local Newspaper Articles Covering Wilson's Announcement, April 7, 1913

Headlines[a]	Source and Newspapers	Number of Times Reprinted	Brief Summary
President Will Appear in Person before Congress, Wilson to Go on Floor of House, President Wilson Will Appear in the Halls of Congress, Wilson Will Deliver His Message in Person, Wilson to Read Own Message, President Will Appear in Person before Congress, Wilson Will Go on Floor and Read Message, President to Read Message to Congress, Wilson to Address Congress Tuesday, Old Precedent to Be Smashed	Associated Press (Article 1): *Times Dispatch* (VA), *Norwich Bulletin* (CT), *Albuquerque Morning Journal* (NM), *Pensacola Journal* (FL), *Calumet News* (MI), *San Francisco Call* (CA), *Arizona Republican* (AZ), *Salt Lake Tribune* (UT), *Daily Missoulian* (MT), *Evening Star* (DC)[b]	10	Setting aside century-old precedents; Congress surprised; Adams precedent; how event will proceed; no queries from Congress; potential for embarrassment[c]
Wilson Astounds Congress Members, President Defends Plan for Message, Wilson Will Read His Own Message, Congress to Hear Wilson on the	Associated Press (Article 2): *Evening Times Republican* (IA), *El Paso Herald* (TX), *Rock Island Argus* (IL), *Evening Times Republican* (IA),	8	Wilson's announcement completely displaces tariff and income tax as chief subjects of popular interest; Adams and Jefferson precedents; Wilson's reasons; congressional surprise

Headline	Newspaper		Description
Floor, President Wilson Will Read His Message to Congress, Wilson's Determination Shocks Old Time Leaders	Evening Times (ND), Evening Standard (UT), Fairmont West Virginian (WV), Albuquerque Evening Herald (NM)		
Wilson Will Read His Tariff Message before Congress	Washington Herald (DC), Sun (NY)	2	Wilson to appear in person; Adams and Jefferson precedents; constitutional warrant; excitement on Capitol Hill; procedure for receiving president
Tariff Bill Calls for Sweeping Cuts, Sixty Third Congress Convenes	United Press: Chickasha Daily (OK)	2	Most sweeping cuts ever attempted; bill has Wilson's approval; Adams precedent; Wilson's reasons
Free List Is Sweeping, Message Will Be Read by Wilson	Associated Press cable: Honolulu Star-Bulletin (HI)	1	One-line mention of Wilson appearing personally
Democrats in Saddle as Extra Session of New Congress Meets	Washington Times (DC)	1	Democratic majorities; one mention of Wilson speaking
Message Will Be Read by Wilson	East Oregonian (OR)	1	Short paragraph; Democrats are pleased
President Will Read His Message	Seattle Star (WA)	1	Short paragraph; Wilson's reasons

[a] Although the headlines varied, the articles were identical.
[b] Includes the first three paragraphs of article 2 (see below); then reprints article 1 in its entirety.
[c] A paragraph about the situation being fraught with potential embarrassment is included in some but not all articles.

Table 4.4: Local Newspaper Articles Covering Wilson's Announcement and Speech, April 8, 1913

Headlines[a]	Source and Newspapers	Number of Times Reprinted	Brief Summary
Wilson's First Message to Be Read in Person, President Wilson Will Appear before Congress, in Person, How Wilson Will Read Message	Associated Press (from April 7): *Ottumwa Tri-Weekly Courier* (IA), *Logan Republican* (UT), *Washington Post* (DC)	3	Wilson's announcement completely displaces tariff and income tax as chief subjects of popular interest; Adams and Jefferson precedents; Wilson's reasons; congressional surprise
Senate Criticises Plan of President to Send Message to Congress, Senators Decry Throne Speech	Associated Press (from April 7): *Washington Herald* (DC), *Sun* (NY)	2	First time in 112 years; criticism from Lodge and Williams
Progressives Will Enliven Extra Session of Congress, Sixty Third Congress in Extra Session, Jefferson Precedent Is Removed, Congress Opened New Session Yesterday, Congress in Session Once More, Breach of Jefferson's Method, Opening of Congress Is Enlivened by the Progressive Party, Wilson Upsets Tradition, Senators Frown on Wilson's Visit	Associated Press (from April 7): *Albuquerque Morning Journal* (NM), *Arizona Republican* (AZ), *Bismarck Daily Tribune* (ND), *Bennington Evening Banner* (VT), *Salt Lake Tribune* (UT), *Norwich Bulletin* (CT)[a], *Pensacola Journal* (FL), *Tulsa Daily World* (OK),	9	Congress's extraordinary session under Democratic domination; Wilson's decision; Jefferson precedent; Williams's deprecation

Newspaper	(no.)	Headline	Comments
Washington Post (DC)		Wilson Will Read Message	Adams and Jefferson precedents; Wilson's reasons; congressional surprise
Associated Press (from April 7): *Hopkinsville Kentuckian* (KY), *Omaha Daily Bee* (NE)	2		
Evening Standard (UT), *Evening Times* (ND), *Topeka State Journal* (KS), *Evening Star* (DC), *El Paso Herald* (TX), *Daily Ardmoreite* (OK), *Albuquerque Evening Herald* (NM)	7	President Reads His Own Message, President Wilson Reads First Message to New Congress Today, Wilson's First Views, Wilson Cheered before He Reads Message in House, Crowd Cheers Wilson in House, Wilson Reads His Message, President Delivers Speech from Throne	Wilson stood on the speaker's rostrum in House; packed galleries; Wilson's arrival[b]
Bridgeport Evening Farmer (CT), *Evening Times Republican* (IA), *Rock Island Argus* (IL)	3	Wilson Dwells Exclusively on Tariff Issue, President Appears before Congress, Wilson Goes to Congress with Views	Revival of old precedent; Wilson reverts to century-old custom, came to Capitol Hill, is a human being[b]
Ocala Evening Star (FL), *Bemidji Daily Pioneer* (MN), *Polk County Observer* (OR)	3	First Message In, Wilson's Message Sticks to Tariff, Wilson's First Message	One-paragraph introduction[b]
Democratic Banner (OH)	1	Goes in Person to Read Message	President to read message in person; Adams precedent; Representative Underwood; agrees with Washington and Adams; Jefferson changes custom

(continued on the next page)

Table 4.4: Continued

Headlines	Source and Newspapers	Number of Times Reprinted	Brief Summary
Congress Breathless as President Wilson Reads His Message	*Washington Times* (DC)	1	History made on Capitol Hill; most remarkable speech ever heard; Wilson's opening; attention to speech[b]
Wilson Personally Reads His Message before Joint Session	*East Oregonian* (OR)	1	Immense crowds; supports Wilson[b] Message before Joint Session
Wilson Sweeps Aside Precedent	United Press leased wire: *Seattle Star* (WA)	1	First time in 112 years
President Wilson Addresses Congress	United Press: *University Missourian* (MO)	1	Lasts only 8 minutes; first time since days of Washington[b]
Congress Awaits Message	*Bisbee Daily Review* (AZ)	1	Political makeup of houses of Congress; Capitol is ready
Democratic Congress Convenes in Special Session	Federal Wireless Telegraph: *Hawaiian Gazette* (HI)	1	Great weather; crowded Capitol; suffragettes; president appeared in person
Wilson Talks to Congress in Person	*Tacoma Times* (WA)	1	Short, descriptive article; includes Wilson's opening remarks
Long Free List and Deep Cuts Stun Democrats	Tribune Bureau: *New York Tribune* (NY)	1	Cold reception for Wilson; detailed description of tariff proposals and potential impact
Wilson Serves Notice in Tariff	Samuel M. Williams:	1	Wilson's entrance; description of scene,

Wilson Serves Notice in Tariff Message He Can't Be Isolated Congress in Session	Samuel M. Williams: *Evening World* (NY) *Deming Graphic* (NM)	1 1	Wilson's entrance; description of scene, speech Short paragraph about opening of Congress and Wilson delivering message

[a]The article in this paper was the same as the others in this group except for a paragraph detailing Senator Williams's objection, which was also mentioned in a subheadline. This article was one of the most overtly critical of Wilson's decision ("Breach of Jefferson's Method, *Norwich Bulletin*, April 8, 1913, 1).
[b]Wilson's full speech was reprinted.

constituted in part of his most active political enemies, somebody might start a diversion that would put him in an embarrassing and undignified position" ("Reading Messages in Person," April 8, 1913, 6). Other accounts supported this interpretation, including one in the *New York Sun* that stated, "Thomas Jefferson's real reason for discontinuing the custom of addressing Congress was that he disliked the idea of speaking and of being questioned by members of Congress" ("Wilson to Read His Own Message," April 7, 1913). Another explanation identified "Jefferson's shortcomings as a public speaker, which made him very sensitive about addressing, particularly, bodies composed largely of experienced orators" ("Finding Precedent for Wilson's Act," *Washington Times*, April 7, 1913, 6).

Republican Henry Cabot Lodge, often referred to as the Senate historian, offered his own explanation of Jefferson's decision when the resolution to invite Wilson to speak was passed. On the Senate floor, Lodge said, "I suppose Mr. Jefferson possibly had the feeling in regard to it that was expressed by his followers and I think he was not, as a rule, much given to speech making" (*Congressional Record*, April 7, 1913, 58). Lodge also read two letters from Jefferson to Congress. The first was Jefferson's explanation of why he was abandoning the custom of his predecessors. In this missive, Jefferson cited the "interests of economy and to relieve Congress from embarrassment."[13] In the second letter, Jefferson explained "more freely that he did it to obviate the 'bloody conflict' that attended the framing of a reply" (*Congressional Record*, April 7, 1913, 58).[14]

Based on these accounts, Jefferson's 1801 decision was reported in 1913 to be primarily a product of the institutional circumstances the president faced, much like those Wilson encountered a century later. Jefferson's desire to avoid partisan conflict in Congress and to usher in his own political ideology, as well as his poor speaking ability, led him to abandon the reading of the annual message to Congress and to provide a written document instead.

Though the 1913 resolution to invite the president to appear before Congress was adopted unanimously, many members expressed reservations ("Senators Frown on Wilson's Visit," *Washington Post*, April 8,

1913, 1). Though both Republican senator Lodge of Massachusetts and Democratic senator John Sharp Williams of Mississippi were critical of the president's proposal, neither opposed the resolution ("Senators Decry Throne Speech," *New York Sun*, April 8, 1913, 1). Despite their reservations, they both made it clear that it was well within the president's rights to deliver a speech. During the Senate's session on April 7, 1913, Williams said in part, "The president is acting both within his right and within his power, and it would be discourteous to oppose it [the resolution]. He [Wilson] has a perfect right to communicate with Congress in either way, either word of mouth or by written message" (*Congressional Record*, 58). Lodge's comments reflected a similar understanding: "It lies wholly with the president to determine as to what method he prefers to communicate with the Houses" (*Congressional Record*, 59). Much of the criticism accused Wilson of abandoning the Republican-Democratic tradition of Jefferson and turning to the Federalist approach of Washington and Adams ("Senators Frown on Wilson's Visit," *Washington Post*, April 8, 1913, 1; "President's Visit Nettles Senators, *New York Times*, April 8, 1913, 1).

Despite these criticisms, and in contrast to some scholars' insistence that Wilson was initiating what amounted to a normative change, any reference to the Constitution supported the president's decision to go to the Capitol, and most suggested that it was a matter of preference. The *Washington Post* noted, "John Adams, George Washington's successor was the last President of the United States to take advantage of this constitutional right" ("Wilson to Read Message in House," April 7, 1913, 1). The *New York Sun* specifically mentioned Article II and observed that "the Constitution lays no restriction or limitation upon the manner in which information and recommendation shall be delivered" ("Wilson to Read His Own Message," April 7, 1913, 1). Even Senator Lodge had to concede that "there was ample constitutional warrant to deliver his message to Congress in person" ("Except Lodge, Senators Approve Wilson's Visit," *Washington Post*, April 10, 1913). Senator Augustus Bacon (D-GA) agreed, stating, "It is the constitutional right of the president to communicate with Congress in such a way as he may himself elect, and it is not for us to determine in what manner he shall do so" (*Congressional Record*, April 7, 1913, 58).

Discussion about Wilson's appearance and, more broadly, the president's role in the legislative process continued in the Capitol in the days following the speech. A number of senators, including James O'Gorman (D-NY) and Benjamin Shively (D-IN), praised Wilson's actions, claiming "it was a deed that showed consideration and real democratic simplicity" and noting that "the president did a thoroughly democratic thing" ("Except Lodge, Senators Approve Wilson's Visit," *Washington Post*, April 10, 1913). As the *Post*'s headline indicates, the protectionist Lodge continued to oppose the president's interference.

The Aftermath of Wilson's Speech

Although there had been some apprehension before the president delivered his speech, many articles indicated that he won over his critics. The *Washington Post* reported on April 9, "There was no doubt that the President's innovation, his return to the customs of the fathers, met with the approval of the great majority of both houses of congress." The *Washington Times* gushed on April 8 that the speech jarred congressmen "from an affected nonchalance and parade of tiredness to a realization of immediate duty to a nation."

One of Wilson's biggest supporters was Democratic stalwart William Jennings Bryan. In his newspaper the *Commoner*, Bryan repeatedly praised Wilson's revival of an old custom and his courage to "risk criticism in doing that which seems to him right, and he did not misjudge the human heart when he decided that the people would approve of his act if he brought himself into closer communications with those public servants who are entrusted with matters of legislation" ("President before Congress," April 18, 1913, 1). Bryan's words suggest that at least some people saw the president's more explicit involvement in the legislative process as a positive development rather than a usurpation.

Bryan also pointed out the important political motivations behind many of the senators' actions. He described the low-tariff senators as "nodding and smiling in approval. But the protectionists were plainly not pleased. Senator Lodge sat bolt upright in his seat and twirled his fingers" ("President Wilson Shattering Precedents and Delighting American People," *Commoner*, April 18, 1913, 1).

In another article, Bryan commented on Roosevelt's relationship with Congress and explained that Roosevelt's demeanor made him less suited to personal appearances on Capitol Hill. Wilson too compared himself to Roosevelt. In a comment to his wife after the speech, the president said, "Wouldn't Teddy have been glad to think of that—I put one over on Teddy and am totally happy" (Berg 2013, 294). Perhaps most tellingly, the *Evening Star* published a cartoon of Theodore Roosevelt with the thought bubble, "Now why didn't I think of that!" (figure 4.2).

Bryan's claims about Wilson were most likely motivated by partisanship, but his praise can be used to illustrate a larger point. Wilson's disposition, his speech-making ability, and the Democrats' control of Congress made this innovation less risky than it might have been for an earlier president. At the same time, Wilson's position as an out-party president trying to consolidate leadership over his partisans and deliver on a campaign promise made the potential reward greater.

Wilson's speech before Congress also attracted more attention than a written speech would have. As newspapers reported, ordinarily the gallery was mostly empty when the clerk read the president's message to Congress. However, the interest generated by Wilson's appearance ensured that "every member should hear his appeal of a thorough revision of the tariff, the sole purpose for which Congress was called into extraordinary session" ("President Reads His Own Message," *New York Evening Post*, April 8, 1913, 1). Even many of the senators recognized how much attention that the president's speech was receiving. Senator Overman (D-NC) said, "I do not recall a President's message which was ever given closer attention" ("President's Address Delights Democrats," *Washington Post*, April 9, 1913, 4).

Figure 4.2. Political cartoon of Theodore Roosevelt appearing in the *Evening Star* on April 8, 1913. (Source: National Archives and Records Administration)

A number of newspaper articles reported that Wilson's appearance and speech were good for American democracy. In particular, the message's brevity and readability made it easy for newspapers across the country to publish it in its entirety rather than carrying just an excerpt, as they often did with longer speeches. Many articles commented that the speech took only eight minutes. In addition, the president's appearance on Capitol Hill and his willingness to be actively involved in the legislative process allowed the public and Congress to view Wilson as a person and not just an institution.

The notion that Congress was out of touch with the public was emphasized in some of the assessments of Wilson's speech. For instance, the *Washington Times* wrote, "Staid Senators and Representatives, strong for the traditions of the dim and musty past, were jarred from an affected nonchalance and parade" ("Congress Breathless as President Wilson Reads His Message," April 8, 1913, 1). A headline in the *Albuquerque Evening Herald* expressed a similar sentiment: "Wilson's Determination to Read Message Shocks Old Time Leaders" (April 7, 1913, 1).

The brevity of the message was seen as a positive attribute:

Nowhere in that hall was there a man inattentive to the words spoken by this new party chieftain. It was the first time in a century that a presidential message had been literally crammed into the minds of those for whom it was intended. And because of the method of delivery and its conciseness and brevity, with not a single essential point omitted, it will be more widely read by the people throughout the country than any message ever sent to Congress. ("Wilson Wins Congress in His Epochal Speech," *Washington Post*, April 9, 1913, 1)

Messages to Congress had become increasingly long and had taken on the format of reports. This made it difficult for newspapers to reprint the messages in their entirety and made it unlikely that either the public or, more importantly, members of Congress would read them thoroughly. In addition, Wilson cleverly devoted the message to one specific topic, rather than a myriad of issues. This allowed the president to focus both Congress and the public on this one policy.

Wilson's final attempt to use public opinion to sway Congress came with his efforts to convince the public to support his Fourteen Points. In the aftermath of World War I, Wilson wanted the United States to become part of the League of Nations. However, deep isolationist tendencies remained in the United States, and Wilson was unable to overcome his opponents in Congress. Building on the examples of Hayes, Harrison, McKinley, and Roosevelt, Wilson took his argument to the people. In this case, Wilson staked out a position with little room for compromise. Ultimately, the tour came to an abrupt end when he suffered a stroke.

An examination of Wilson's decision to deliver a speech in person to Congress for the first time in more than one hundred years highlights the influence of outside forces on popular presidential communication. There was little commentary suggesting that Wilson's decision violated a constitutional norm, and the evidence suggests that circumstances more than ideology encouraged the president to embark on this innovation.[15] In fact, the practice of addressing Congress in person was not consolidated until Franklin D. Roosevelt some twenty years later.[16] And even then, presidents occasionally sent Congress written documents (Peters and Woolley 2021).

Finally, when Wilson decided to take the United States into World War I after years of isolation, he chose the newspaper as his preferred method of communication. At this point, a speech printed in the newspaper would reach most of the country within a few days. Wilson kept the message relatively brief so that it could be reprinted in its entirety. "Address to the American People" appeared initially in the *Washington Post* on April 16, 1917, before being reprinted in newspapers nationwide. Wilson's choice in this case shows that written and spoken rhetoric sometimes served the same purpose, and the newspaper was still the only way to reach the public as a whole. However, once presidents realized the power of radio and later television, written communication was relegated to a secondary role for the remainder of the twentieth century.

Conclusion

Wilson's decision to reintroduce the practice of addressing Congress in person was the result of decades of evolution in presidential rhetoric; it was not simply the product of Wilson's leadership philosophy. Evidence shows that the content of presidential rhetoric began to change long before Wilson's election. The roots of going public were clearly present in the actions of the post–Civil War presidents, including Hayes and Harrison, who toured the country extensively and discussed pressing national issues with the American public. McKinley and Roosevelt took this strategy to the next level, and the newspapers of the day identified their rhetorical activities as going over the heads of Congress and appealing directly to the people, the very definition of going public. Wilson, looking to unite a fractured Democratic Party and to focus both press and public attention on the tariff issue, took advantage of the opportunities presented to him. Importantly, these opportunities were created by forces outside of the president's control, including a changing media environment, weakening political parties, and the rise of pluralism. These changes provided incentives for presidents to reach out directly to the American public.

5

5

Going National: Warren G. Harding to
George H. W. Bush, 1922–1992

The "going national" period encompasses the longest and most unusual media environment in presidential history. For most of this era, polarization was relatively low, objective reporting was the norm, most media outlets had high barriers to entry, and presidents could reach most of the nation with relative ease through radio or television. These structural factors encouraged presidents to view the American people as a whole as the persuadable public.[1]

Structural Factors

Polarization can be described on two levels: among elites and within the electorate. One well-established way of measuring polarization in Congress is through DW nominate scores (Lewis et al. 2022).[2] As figure 5.1 shows, the period between approximately 1920 and 1990 represented lower levels of party polarization in part because of the presence of southern Democrats, but also because Republican members of Congress were more moderate. Pew Research Center (2014) shows a similar phenomenon in the electorate, but without the same historical context.

The communication landscape was on the precipice of a significant

Figure 5.1. Distance between party means (the mean of each party's ideological distribution), 1880–2016. (Source: Lewis et al. 2022)

innovation that would, for the first time, give the president a truly national audience. Warren G. Harding (1921–1923) was the first president with access to the radio, although the new technology was in its infancy when he took office. The first scheduled political broadcast took place on election night 1920, when only one in five hundred families had radios. Twenty years later, 80 percent of American families had radios in their homes (Craig 2003). Networks tried to remain nonpartisan, but they treated broadcasts by administration officials as a public service during nonelection times. This policy allowed administration voices to dominate nonelection periods and added a powerful new advantage to incumbency (Craig 2003). Barriers to entry in this media environment were relatively high, resulting in less competition for the public's attention than would be the case by the end of the century. The creation of a national audience with objective standards of reporting had consequences for presidential rhetoric, as I examine in this chapter. I also discuss incentives for more frequent communication such as the enfranchisement of women, the on-

going professionalization of journalism, and the diminishing strength of
political parties.

The Press Conference

One consequence of the increasing professionalism of journalists was the
establishment of the press conference. Reporters had gained a permanent
position in the White House with the creation of a pressroom during
Theodore Roosevelt's 1902 renovation (Cornwell 1979; Tebbel and Watts
1985). Woodrow Wilson was the first president to hold regular press conferences, although the reporters were not supposed to quote him directly
(Tebbel and Watts 1985; Ryfe 1999; Ponder 1998). However, Wilson became disenchanted with the press and ended the practice long before his
term ran out (Kumar 2010).

Harding conducted off-the-record meetings with members of the
press and resumed the twice-weekly press conferences that Wilson had
abandoned (Kumar 2010). The first of these press conferences occurred
on March 22, 1921, and was covered on the front page of the next day's
New York Times. The president took questions, in writing, and discussed
his cabinet meeting. Reporters could not quote Harding directly, but the
public quickly figured out that the "White House spokesman" was the
president himself (Pollard 1947). The resumption of press conferences garnered Harding praise from the press and an opportunity to direct public
attention toward political affairs, ·a task that had become more complicated in the twentieth century, as concerns related to industrialization and
urbanization threatened to take center stage (Schudson 2001; Ryfe 2005).

It was during the Harding administration that the press conference
became regular and permanent, significantly increasing the frequency of
popular presidential communication. An "examination of the *New York
Times* during the first three months of the Harding administration suggests both the importance of the conference as [a] link between President
and public and the relative success that Harding had in 'making news'

Table 5.1: Presidential Press Conferences, Wilson through Trump

President	Number[a]
Wilson	159
Harding	Unknown[b]
Coolidge	407
Hoover	268
FDR	881
Truman	324
Eisenhower	193
JFK	65
LBJ	135
Nixon	39
Ford	40
Carter	59
Reagan	46
G. H. W. Bush	137
Clinton	193
G. W. Bush	210
Obama	164
Trump	24

[a]I used the American Presidency Project for these estimates. For slightly different numbers, see Kumar (2005).

[b]We know that Harding spoke with reporters, but there is no count of press conferences (Kumar 2005).

and keeping presidential activities in the limelight" (Cornwell 1979, 65). Table 5.1 shows the number of recorded presidential press conferences from Wilson through Trump.

When Harding died on August 2, 1923, Calvin Coolidge became the sixth vice president to assume the presidency. Coolidge institutionalized the twice-weekly press conference that Harding had resumed. On Tuesdays and Fridays the president met with reporters and answered questions, which were written and submitted to him in advance. Again, the press could not quote the president directly but instead referred to a White House spokesman. Coolidge "put press conferences on a schedule, to solicit press backing for his administration, generously giving them news and hoping that on their side the press would respond with sympathetic stories" (Quint and Ferrell 1964, 20). Coolidge gave 407 press conferences during his time in office, representing almost 80 percent of his total spoken rhetoric.

· Coolidge used these press conferences for a number of purposes, including to make announcements about upcoming trips, nominations, and occasionally major policy decisions (Quint and Ferrell 1964). As the president himself described, "Sometimes I made an appeal direct [*sic*] to the country by stating my position at the newspaper conferences" (quoted in Quint and Ferrell 1964, 223). Coolidge understood that meeting with reporters allowed him to tell his side of the story, and he realized that "he himself could never have composed such skillful accounts of his administration for verbatim or background release to the country's newspapers. It was far easier and much more effective, to meet the correspondents twice a week and let them do the work" (Quint and Ferrell 1964, 1).

Unlike other presidents, Coolidge even took the press on vacation with him, unwilling to allow any pause in information about the president or the administration. Also unlike his predecessors, Coolidge seemed to encourage press scrutiny of his private life, viewing it positively and as a way to maintain the public's interest in him (Cornwell 1957). Coolidge's relatively high frequency of communication was attributable in part to his commitment to regular press conferences.

As table 5.1 shows, although the number of press conferences conducted by each president has varied significantly, presidents in the early twentieth century spoke to the press quite often.

Rise of the Radio

The advent of the radio gave presidents their first real opportunity to speak to the nation as a whole and allowed the public to hear the president's words simultaneously. On April 4, 1923, Harding had the distinction of becoming the first president to be heard over national radio, although some of his speeches had been broadcast on local stations over the past two years. As the *New York Times* reported, the radio allowed Harding to address the largest audience in history ("Radio: Mr. Harding to Broadcast," April 8, 1923, E4).

Moreover, the radio created opportunities for broadening political participation and extending the president's message to some of the newly enfranchised. In the early 1920s, women voters might have found it difficult to "hear the candidates," perhaps being reluctant to attend "the great mass meetings because of the crowds and lack of seating capacity in halls and auditoriums" (Sullivan 1924, 19). However, the radio eliminated this issue, making it possible for anyone to listen to political speeches from the comfort of their living room. In fact, "with radio interesting great additional groups of citizens in the affairs of government, many organizations are pushing a 'Get-Out-the-Vote' campaign" (Sullivan 1924, 22). Radio also made participation in politics less demanding for many citizens because they could listen to politicians from the comfort of their homes, and in a democracy, deeper involvement by a larger portion of the public is a positive development.

When Harding set out on his western tour in the summer of 1923, his speeches were scheduled to be broadcast over the radio. This innovation meant that Harding had to stand in front of a microphone while speaking instead of moving around the stage, which changed his style of oratory and made his delivery less effective ("Cordial to Harding, Cold to Speeches," *New York Times*, June 25, 1923, 2).

After Harding died and Coolidge became president, he gave at least five nationally broadcast speeches and another three speeches broadcast over local (New York and/or Washington) stations between his message to Congress in December 1923 and the convention in June 1924 (Craig 2003). Coolidge strategically chose events that were nonpartisan, including a eulogy of Harding, a Memorial Day speech, and a discussion of the movement for better homes, in an effort to ingratiate himself with the public (Craig 2003). Addressing the nation in this way would have quite difficult through the newspaper.

Radio had other implications for politics and democracy. One journalist speculated that the radio would speed up a politician's ability to
leverage popular support and would prioritize new skills, including "having a radio personality" as opposed to the more traditional rhetorical
skills required when speaking in front of an audience (Sullivan 1924, 20).
At the 1924 conventions, the acceptance speeches of both parties' presidential nominees were broadcast on the radio for the first time. Instead of
delivering their acceptance speeches in the afternoon (between 3:00 and
5:00 p.m.), when the greatest number of people would be there in person,
the addresses were given at 8:00 p.m., when the radio audience would be
the largest (Sullivan 1924).

In 1925 Coolidge became the first president whose inaugural address
was broadcast over the radio, reaching twenty-two million people over a
network of twenty-five stations (Craig 2003). He also used the medium
about once a month to speak to the public directly. Despite the "Silent
Cal" moniker, Coolidge "was a communicator when it mattered, and he
turned out to be the most adroit manipulator of the media since Theodore Roosevelt" (Tebbel and Watts 1985, 403). That nickname arose
from Coolidge's aversion to small talk and his tendency to be reserved in
private conversation, but he was widely acknowledged as a gifted public
speaker (Prosper 1961, 6). In fact, the *New York Times* pushed back on
the idea of Silent Cal, noting that "the President is anything but silent,
radio can prove" ("President's Unseen Audience Equal to the Population in 1865," September 4, 1927, XX11). The newspaper even compared
Coolidge's twenty-eight radio speeches to Wilson's seventeen, labeling
the latter "remarkably silent." Of course, the radio was in its infancy when
Wilson was president, so this comparison was problematic.

In a comparison with Theodore Roosevelt, the *New York Times* wrote
that Coolidge "has, in fact, spoken to more of his countrymen than any
president in history," estimating that the president's audience of thirty
million exceeded the population of the country in 1865. And the paper
explained why radio mattered so much: "Notwithstanding the fact that
the President's speech is always in the newspaper following his address,

and there is concrete evidence that it is carefully read by hundreds of thousands, nevertheless four-fifths of the letters received at the White House indicate that the writers actually heard the president. As more territory is covered by radio stations more letters and telegrams are received" ("President's Unseen Audience Equal to the Population in 1865," *New York Times*, September 4, 1927, XX11).

As important as the radio was for Coolidge, it was not yet ubiquitous, and newspapers remained a vital method of communication with the public.[3] Seventy percent of Coolidge's addresses and messages were published in newspapers across the country, as had been the case since Washington's presidency (Wallace 2008, 1). Many of these speeches were directed to interest groups and covered topics such as foreign policy, taxes, and agricultural policy. Only about forty speeches were delivered over the radio, and these addresses tended to include broadly appealing topics, such as remarks congratulating Charles Lindbergh ("President's Unseen Audience Equal to the Population in 1865," *New York Times*, September 4, 1927, XX11; Lewis 1992).

In the wake of both Wilson's and Harding's physically grueling and ultimately deadly tours, Coolidge was urged to see the radio as an alternative "to conserve his health and reach a greater number of people." Eugene McDonald, founder of Zenith Radio, wrote the president a long letter extolling the virtues of the radio, which included fewer physical demands than touring and the ability to reach a huge audience (fifteen million). The president's secretary "assured the broadcasters that their suggestion would be acted upon at the earliest possible moment" ("Coolidge to Talk by Radio," *New York Times*, November 29, 1923, 1).

Coolidge identified another advantage of the radio, noting that speaking from the rear platforms of trains was ineffective because "the confusion is so great that few people could hear and it does not seem to me very dignified" (Coolidge 1929, 218). Presidential tours often generated crowds numbering in the thousands, making it difficult for attendees to hear the president and therefore diminishing the effectiveness of his speech. Moreover, some speculated that the radio benefited Coolidge

because of the "unimpressiveness of his physical appearance" (Sullivan 1924, 21). In his memoir, Senator James E. Watson (R-IN) recalled
Coolidge telling him: "I am very fortunate to have come in with the radio. I can't make an engaging, rousing or oratorical speech to [a] crowd
like you can." However, the president noted that he had "a good radio
voice" and could "get my message across to them without acquainting
them with my lack of oratorical ability" (Watson 1936, 239). This example
highlights how a president's personal skills may encourage him to take
advantage of certain innovations while avoiding others.

Another Exception: Herbert Hoover (1929–1933)

Herbert Hoover seemed well prepared to be president when he was
elected in 1928. As commerce secretary, Hoover had gained a reputation
for his accessibility to the press, and the excitement was palpable when
two hundred newspaper correspondents attended his first press conference on March 6, 1929. However, as president, Hoover retreated from
journalists, although he changed the policy about quoting the president
directly, which had long frustrated reporters ("The Press and the President," *New York Times*, March 7, 1929, 17).

Hoover was exasperated by the press's attention to what he considered trivial matters, including his family and their "ways" (Nelson 1998,
746). Leaks to the press led Hoover to limit the information journalists
received, which only exacerbated the situation because they viewed
this move as censorship by the administration (Nelson 1998). Pressure
mounted on Hoover to keep up communications with the public because
the American people were used to hearing from the president regularly.
The Seventy-First Congress increased the demands on the president by
broadcasting more than one hundred "addresses in explanation of and
for and against pending measures." By the end of the year, one-third of
senators and fifty representatives had discussed legislation over the air
("Legislators Establish New Record for Appearances before Microphone,"

New York Times, August 17, 1930, 117). In addition, Hoover's cabinet members spoke regularly to the public (Becker 1961). Despite his reluctance, Hoover delivered one hundred radio addresses, or an average of about twenty-three per year, during his time in office ("Talking to the People," *New York Times*, March 19, 1933, X8).

The president's unwillingness to work with the press greatly hindered his ability to lead the country through the greatest economic crisis of the century. By 1932, Hoover had become openly hostile to the press, and an aide stated flatly in his diary that the president hated the press (Nelson 1998, 45). The administration's inability to maintain a working relationship with the press complicated everything about Hoover's presidency.

Radio Maximized: Franklin D. Roosevelt (1933–1945)

Radio featured prominently in the 1932 campaign between Republican incumbent Hoover and Democrat Franklin D. Roosevelt, the governor of New York. One important consequence was that the candidates had to give speeches that appealed to the whole nation, rather than a local audience. In the past, it had been customary to give essentially the same speech, simply tailoring certain aspects of it to whatever town or city they were in. Hoover's speeches focused on defending his administration in what proved to be a remarkably ineffective campaign against the charismatic Roosevelt, who offered the country a new direction (Carcasson 1998).

With any technological innovation, it takes time for people to adopt it and to perfect its use. Roosevelt was far from the first president to use the radio, but it was during his administration that it reached its full potential as a tool for communicating with the people. Roosevelt used the radio to lead Americans through two of the worst crises in the country's history: the Great Depression and World War II. Unlike his predecessor Hoover, who ignored advice to speak directly to listeners rather than simply reading his speeches, Roosevelt "spoke slowly and with the simplest and clear-

**The Frequency of Popular Presidential Communication
Compared to % of Homes with Radios per Year:
Wilson to Truman**

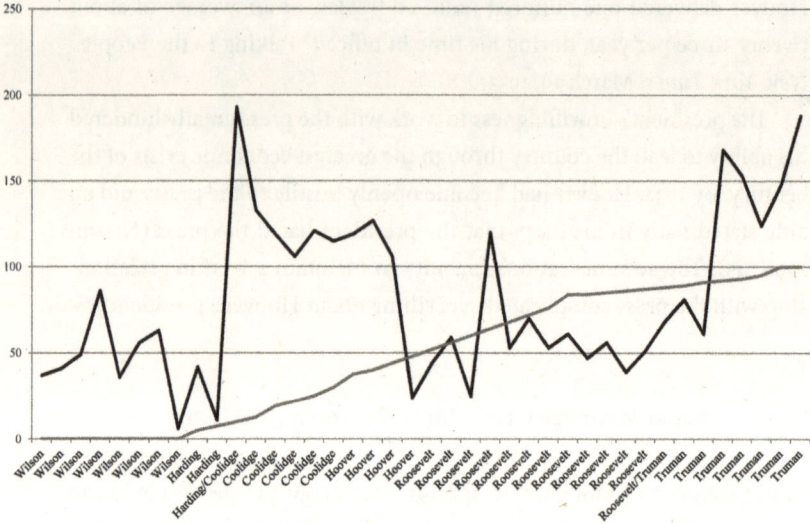

Figure 5.2. Frequency of popular presidential communication compared to percentage of households with radios: Wilson through Truman (Source: US Census 1971)

est possible language" (Craig 2003, 155). FDR's effective use of the radio was essential to his ability to reconstruct American politics.

As president, Roosevelt used the radio to reach the people directly, mobilize public opinion, and hide his disability (Ryfe 1999; Craig 2003). FDR had watched Hoover's struggle to use the radio effectively and Coolidge's relative success with the new medium, and he incorporated his predecessors' most effective communication strategies into his own approach. Of course, by the time Roosevelt became president, radios were everywhere.

Roosevelt's skillful use of the radio encouraged people to contact their congressional representatives in record numbers and "assist[ed] in making the heralded new deal a success" ("Talking to the People," *New York*

Times, March 19, 1933, X8; Ryfe 1999). Roosevelt was able to introduce an intimacy into the relationship between the president and the people that had not existed before. Overall, however, Roosevelt communicated less frequently than many of his predecessors in part because of his strategic use of the radio and in part because of his physical disability, which prevented him from going on long tours. Radio made this kind of all-day speech making, as the president's train traveled from stop to stop, obsolete. Figure 5.2 shows the frequency of popular presidential communication compared to the number radios per household from Wilson through Truman.[4] During this time, the trend toward more frequent presidential speech continued, but unevenly, suggesting that although radio created a national audience for the president, the new technology was not responsible for the increased frequency of presidential speech.

By the 1930s, most Americans had radios in their homes. On March 12, 1933, Roosevelt gave his first fireside chat to the nation and began by saying, "I want to talk a few minutes with the people of the United States about banking." It was incredibly well received by the public, and only a few days into his administration, Roosevelt was already being called the "Radio President" ("Talking to the People," *New York Times*, March 19, 1933, X8). The radio allowed him to reach the American people and reassure them on many of the pressing issues of the day. These chats, each of which focused on only one issue, were intended to be "informal, simple presentations to be listened to and comprehended by the great mass of American voters" (Braden and Brandenburg 1955, 292). The president generally spoke for fifteen to forty-five minutes between 9:00 and 11:00 p.m. to reach the most people and hold their interest.

The connection between FDR and the people was clear in the public's response. In the first twelve days of his administration, the White House received fourteen thousand telegrams responding to Roosevelt's communications and his policies ("Topics of the Times," *New York Times*, March 18, 1933, 12). By the end of Roosevelt's first year in office, the White House had hired a night shift to deal with all the mail (Biser 2016). Almost immediately, members of Congress felt the effects of the power

Roosevelt commanded through the radio, as constituents reached out to express their support for the president ("Talking to the People," *New York Times*, March 19, 1933, X8). As *New York Times* correspondent Arthur Krock reported, the president's ability to appeal to the people through the radio gave him new power. In an effort to expedite passage of an economic bill, Roosevelt spoke on the radio to build support for a measure to allow beer sales. Krock wrote that members of Congress would no doubt "hear from home a chorus which will drown out the calls of the veterans' and civil servants' lobbies to emasculate the economy measure" ("Beer Move Hailed as Strategic Coup," *New York Times*, March 14, 1933, 2). This observation illustrates the importance of technological innovation to the president's ability to go public. As much as earlier presidents may have wanted to press policy issues with the people, they were constrained by forces entirely outside their control (and unrelated to their understanding of the Constitution).

By 1948, 95 percent of American homes were equipped with radios, and radio played an integral role in Harry S. Truman's victory. Newspapers overwhelmingly supported his opponent Thomas Dewey, and Truman's campaign advisers believed that "radio [was] crucial to getting the Democratic message across to voters without having it filtered through newspaper bias" (Carroll 1987, 121). Moreover, it was estimated that fewer than a million Americans ever attended a campaign rally or saw one of the candidates speak in person, making radio critical (Summers n.d.). From January to June, "practically every address delivered by a presidential candidate was carried on a coast-to-coast radio hookup" (Summers n.d., 434).

Television

Television was still in its infancy when Truman became president after FDR's death in 1945. The new president's 1946 annual message was initially scheduled to be broadcast on television, but in the end, the House clerk read it to Congress. This development provoked little comment in the *New York Times* ("Truman to Send Message to Congress for Reading," January 10, 1946, 16). A number of Truman's speeches were televised on local stations in New York and Washington, DC ("Truman Talk Televised," *New York Times*, April 22, 1947, 14). Television would not reach meaningful audiences until the middle of the next decade, but its ability to change how people experienced presidential rhetoric was clear from the beginning. When Truman's November 1947 message to Congress was televised, the *New York Times* observed that, for watchers, "the occasion was real to them as it was not for those who merely listened." The article concluded by stating: "Television is young. When it grows up an entire nation will see as well as hear great distant figures and events. Democracy will again be a town meeting. May it take strength from this invention" ("History in Television," *New York Times*, November 18, 1947, 28).

Television did not necessarily add to the president's national audience, but it did add a new visual dimension and resulted in renewed public attention (Ragsdale 1987). Both the Republican and Democratic National Conventions were broadcast on live TV for the first time in 1956, and as many as fifty million Americans watched, drawn by the novelty of seeing the presidential candidates chosen (Gilbert 1986).

Both political parties asked Dwight D. Eisenhower to run for president in 1952, but the popular former general chose to run as a Republican to break the one-party dominance that he viewed as detrimental to the country. Eisenhower served at a time when the Cold War became a central part of American life. During his presidency and afterward, Eisenhower remained very popular with the American public (O'Gorman 2008).

The *New York Times* reported on April 29, 1956, that radio and television were critical for Eisenhower, especially after he had a heart attack in September 1955. In the same article, the Eisenhower reelection campaign announced that he would make no whistle-stop train trips and instead would rely on "mass communications to get his message to the voters" ("Campaign Special: Train or TV," *New York Times*, April 29, 1956, 237).

Eisenhower was a "master user of the U.S. mass media" (Allen 1993, 6).
His TV firsts included the first televised fireside chat, first TV news conference, first televised cabinet meeting, first presidential TV consultant,
and first White House TV studio (Allen 1993, 8). Many of these firsts
can be attributed to timing. More than half of Americans had access to
television by the mid-1950s, and it made sense for Eisenhower to use his
popularity with the public to push his agenda forward.

The Golden Age of Presidential Communication

Television added visual interest to presidential speeches. By 1960, 87 percent of American homes (more than forty-six million) had TVs—a 25
percent increase over 1956 (Watson 1994). Now the public could both see
and hear the president. Scholars have labeled 1960–1980 the golden age
of presidential communication because of that period's unique media environment (Baum and Kernell 1999). This golden age was characterized
by a small number of TV channels, which had high barriers to entry and
gave the president access to a national audience whenever he wanted.

Although Eisenhower appeared on TV regularly, it was John F. Kennedy who mastered the medium. With his good looks and quick wit,
Kennedy skillfully leveraged the new medium to consolidate his popularity after a narrow electoral victory (Scheele 1989). Kennedy's live televised press conference, the first of its kind for an American president,
was watched by sixty-one million Americans. The *New York Times* reported that Kennedy's team changed the time of the press conference to
6:00 p.m. to "reach a larger radio and TV audience" ("News of TV and Radio," January 22, 1961, X11). *New York Times* journalist Jack Gould hailed
the new time slot as "eminently sensible and constructive" and noted that
"any procedure that permits a closer liaison between the average citizen
and Washington surely is desirable and last night in the living room there
was a feeling of participation that had not existed before" ("TV: Sensible
Innovation," January 26, 1961, 59). Fellow journalist Arthur Krock pointed

**The Frequency of Popular Presidential Communication
Compared to % of Homes with TV per Year:
Truman to Carter**

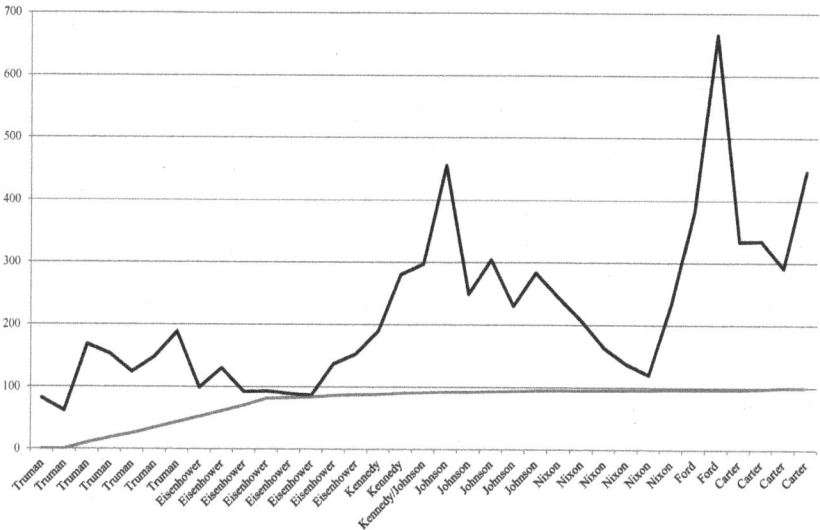

Figure 5.3. Frequency of popular presidential communication compared to percentage of households with TV: Truman through Carter (Source: "Number of TV Households in America 1950–1978," *American Century*, accessed July 14, 2022, https://americancentury.omeka.wlu.edu/items/show/136)

out the pitfalls of a live press conference, as opposed to the taped and edited versions televised in the past: "The advance to live television automatically destroyed this historic safeguard of Presidents, because the function of editing ends with publication." However, Krock found that, given Kennedy's "poise, competence and demonstrated sense of the enormous responsibility of the President," he was up to the challenge ("Three Who Had Been There Before," *New York Times*, January 27, 1961, 22).

During his almost three years as president, Kennedy's press conferences averaged eighteen million viewers (Scheele 1989). Kennedy took advantage of his skill and addressed the public often, accounting for the next significant increase in the frequency of popular presidential communication. As figure 5.3 shows, TV reached its maturity rather quickly, but it is unlikely that it was responsible for this increase. Although TV made it easier to reach a national audience, other factors led to the increased frequency of popular presidential communication.

One of these factors was likely another new technology Kennedy had at his disposal: Air Force One. FDR was the first president to fly, but he used an ordinary military plane commissioned for presidential travel (Ellis 2008). Both Truman and Eisenhower had propeller planes. Eisenhower flew more than twice as many miles as Truman, but a majority of those miles came in the last year of his presidency, when he traveled in a Boeing 707 jet. In 1962, Kennedy got a new custom-made Boeing 707 that flew almost twice as fast as its predecessor and could travel seven thousand miles before needing to refuel (Ellis 2008, 222). Air Force One allowed presidents to reach the public more quickly and safely than ever. Over the next sixty years, presidents steadily increased their domestic travel in efforts to promote their legislative agendas in an increasingly competitive media environment (Kernell [1986] 1997; Rottinghaus 2010).

Speaking to Congress or the People?

The annual message and State of the Union address had been important ways for presidents to communicate their policy priorities since the late eighteenth century, and television provided a new opportunity to reach a national audience. Lyndon B. Johnson tried to capitalize on this opportunity by moving his State of the Union address to the evening in an effort to attract a larger audience and promote his Great Society reforms.[5] This strategic use of the State of the Union leaves no doubt that LBJ's speech was addressed to both Congress and the public, but what about presidents before him? As illustrated in earlier chapters, presidents including Jackson, Cleveland, and Hayes cited the public as part of the audience for their annual messages. Moreover, annual messages were printed and reprinted in newspapers nationwide and were the subject of editorial commentary for days if not weeks. In sum, these findings cast doubt on Tulis's (1987) hypothesis that nineteenth-century presidential rhetoric was addressed primarily to Congress as opposed to the public. There is little evidence that Wilson was single-handedly responsible for a change in audience.[6]

Here, I perform one more empirical test and examine the intended audience of the annual message or State of the Union address by looking at the speech's opening. If Wilson ushered in a constitutional change in the president's audience, we should see changes in the way his annual message, one of the most visible pieces of presidential rhetoric, was cast. However, as table 5.2 shows, this change takes place much later. Prior to 1959, the State of the Union was addressed to "Fellow Citizens of the Senate and House of Representatives," "Members of Congress," or some variation thereof, despite the fact that all these speeches were published in newspapers and, from 1921 on, many were broadcast over the radio. Eisenhower's 1959 address was the first to mention "my fellow citizens," and not until 1969 were "my fellow Americans" included at the beginning of every annual message or State of the Union address. This analysis shows that presidents did not include the public in their salutations until much later than is often thought. Even so, it would be hard to argue that citizens were not part of the intended audience long before the 1960s. The purpose of this observation is to caution against making assumptions about presidential rhetoric without delving into the historical context.

LBJ and his successor, Richard Nixon, would test the American people's belief in the presidency and in the media. Newscaster Walter Cronkite was famously known as the most trusted man in America, but after Vietnam and Watergate, faith in the media fell.

The Great Communicator: Ronald Reagan (1981–1989)

Ronald Reagan presents an interesting dilemma for my efforts to identify the president's intended audience. In many ways, Reagan fits seam-

Table 5.2: Salutations in Annual Messages, George Washington through Lyndon B. Johnson

Salutation	President (Dates of Annual Message)
Fellow Citizens of the Senate and House of Representatives	Washington (1790–1796); Jefferson (1801); Madison (1809–1816); Monroe (1817–1824); J. Q. Adams (1825–1828); Jackson (1829–1836); Van Buren (1837–1840); Polk (1845–1848); Taylor (1849); Fillmore (1850–1852); Pierce (1853–1856); Buchanan (1857–1860); Lincoln (1861–1864); A. Johnson (1865–1868); Hayes (1877–1880)
Gentlemen of the Senate and Gentlemen of the House of Representatives	J. Adams (1797–1800)
To the Senate and House of Representatives	Jefferson (1802–1808); Grant (1869–1876); B. Harrison (1889–1892); McKinley (1897–1900); T. Roosevelt (1901–1908); Taft (1910–1912); Wilson (1919); Hoover (1929–1932)
To the Senate and House of Representatives of the United States	Tyler (1841–1844); Arthur (1881–1884)
To the Congress of the United States	Cleveland (1885–1888, 1893–1896); Coolidge (1924); Truman (1946); Eisenhower (1957, 1961)
Gentlemen of the Congress	Wilson (1913–1918, 1920)
To the Congress	FDR (1944–1945);

Mr. Speaker and Members of Congress	Harding (1921)
Members of Congress	Harding (1922);
	Coolidge (1925–1928)
Mr. President, Mr. Speaker, Senators and	FDR (1934)
Representatives in Congress	
Mr. President, Mr. Speaker, Members of the	FDR (1935–1940)
Senate and of the House of Representatives	
Mr. President, Mr. Speaker, Members of the	Truman (1947);
Congress of the United States	Eisenhower (1953–1956,
	1958, 1960);
	Kennedy (1961, 1963)
Mr. Speaker, Mr. Vice President,	LBJ (1967)
distinguished Members of the Congress	
Mr. President, Mr. Speaker, Members of the	Eisenhower (1959)
Eighty-Sixth Congress, my fellow citizens	
Mr. Vice President, my old colleague from	Kennedy (1962)
Massachusetts and your new Speaker,	
John McCormack, Members of the	
Eighty-Seventh Congress, ladies and	
gentlemen	
Mr. Speaker, Mr. President, Members of the	LBJ (1964–1966, 1968–1969)
House and Senate, my fellow Americans	
No salutation	Taft (1909);
	Coolidge (1923);
	FDR (1942)

lessly into the "going national" era; however, change was under way. And although it did not hinder Reagan's ability to lead, his success made it more difficult for those who followed, especially his immediate successor, George H. W. Bush.

The media dubbed Reagan the "Great Communicator" early in his presidency because of his skill in dealing with key elites, including the media (King and Schudson 1995). Though there is some scholarly debate about Reagan's ability to sway public opinion, there is no doubt that his affability enhanced his popularity with the American public (King and Schudson 1995; Hertsgaard 1988). Similarly, some of his opponents claimed that Reagan was the "Teflon" president because his personal popularity seemed impervious to criticism (Lanoue 1989). Rhetorical scholar Paul D. Erickson (1985) argues that Reagan's ability to turn politics into stories was his most powerful rhetorical tool. Today, Reagan's legacy as a masterful orator endures.

Reagan was likable and put his skills as an actor to good use when delivering speeches, but he and his team also understood the power of the press. Reagan's communication team had a sophisticated strategy to "transform it [the press] into an unwitting mouthpiece of the government" (Hertsgaard 1988, 5). David Gergen, Reagan's communications director, notes that of the six presidents he served, only Reagan saw the press as an ally. He attributes Reagan's successful relationship to two factors: the president's respect for the press corps, and the active approach Reagan's communications team took in courting the American public (Gergen 2001, 185).

Reagan's communications team enjoyed a significant advantage that does not exist today: it was operating at the height of the age of broadcast news (Williams and Delli Carpini 2011). Gergen and his people were able to control what information came out of the White House and, more importantly, how that information was reported. As Gergen notes, "I worked hard under Reagan to persuade the press corps that he was on the right track, often calling television correspondents just before they went on the air and to make sure our views were represented in their stories" (2001, 187). The story line for Reagan was simple: he was a new protagonist in the White House battling the entrenched congressional establishment (King and Schudson 1995, 144). Reagan's successful mobilization of the New Right contributed to this narrative.

As I show in the next chapter, by the end of the Reagan administration, the golden age of presidential communication was ending. The rise of talk radio, cable TV, and eventually the internet would splinter the president's audience in the 1990s. By the turn of the twenty-first century, reaching the American public as a whole would be an increasingly difficult task.

Conclusion

Beginning in the 1920s and extending into the 1980s, presidents enjoyed access to the American public in a way that was unparalleled in US history. The radio and then television allowed the president's words to be broadcast into American homes, and Air Force One allowed the president to travel the country with ease. Importantly, professional journalists were relatively friendly to the president during this time, and objectivity was the norm. Moreover, access to communications technology was quite limited. For most of this period, there were only a handful of national broadcast channels. For the most part, the American people were interested in what the president had to say, and even if they were not, it was difficult to avoid him.

The 1960s–1980s represented the zenith of presidential rhetoric before a national audience (Baum and Kernell 1999; Young and Perkins 2005). Millions of Americans watched Kennedy's first live televised press conferences, and presidents used major national addresses as their primary means of public communication (Scheele 1989; Coe and Neumann 2011). When Presidents Nixon, Ford, and Carter gave major addresses or press conferences on television, they could expect almost half of the American people to be watching (Wattenberg 2004). Presidents could expect their addresses to be broadcast on network TV to a large national audience, and what they had to say would dominate the news cycle for days to come (Baum and Kernell 2006; Scacco and Coe 2016). However, as I discuss in the next chapter, this golden age did not last, and it may have created artificial and unrealistic expectations of how persuasive a president can hope to be.

6

Going Targeted: William Clinton to Donald J. Trump, 1993–2021

The media landscape that emerged in the last part of the twentieth century was in some ways similar to that of the mid-nineteenth century. Beginning in the 1980s and accelerating through the rest of the century, news sources multiplied and became increasingly partisan. Though highly polarized, political parties were also weak, leading to an increasing focus on personality and the continued proliferation of popular presidential communication in an effort to "break through the noise" (Eshbaugh-Soha and Peake 2011). Given these circumstances, it became significantly harder for presidents to reach members of the public who did not already support them, so they turned to mobilizing supporters as a primary communication strategy. For that reason, I call this era of presidential communication "going targeted." It has become increasingly rare for presidents to address the nation; instead, they turn to microaudiences of supporters.

A Fragmented Media Landscape

By the 1990s, consumers of news media had many choices. Cable news had grown significantly; CNN began broadcasting in 1980, and Fox News and MSNBC launched in 1996 (Hemmer 2016). As channels proliferated, so did soft news, which led to less coverage of the president. At the same time, information about the president became increasingly negative and cynical (Cohen 2008, xi; Ragsdale 1984, 1987). Talk radio, which got its start in the late 1980s and 1990s, was in full bloom by the 2010s, with more than thirty-five hundred all-talk or all-news stations. Though originally somewhat ideologically diverse, by 2011, talk radio was overwhelming conservative (Sobieraj and Berry 2011). This growth in news sources splintered the public. Moreover, the growing number of cable TV channels and, more recently, streaming services made it possible for citizens to avoid news altogether if they chose (Baum and Kernell 1999; Cohen 2008). These forces combined to create a situation in which "the major networks no longer offer presidents access to a common space where all Americans gather on a routine basis" (Baum and Kernell 1999, 188). This made it nearly impossible for presidents to access, much less persuade those Americans who disagreed with them. In sum, "whereas presidents once built a public leadership strategy that placed considerable weight on leading the broad mass public, they now place marginally less emphasis on leading the broad mass public and more on mobilizing narrower segments of the populace" (Cohen 2008, xii).

Accordingly, scholars found that despite the steadily increasing frequency of speech, presidents had little ability to move public opinion (Edwards 2006). In response, presidents gave fewer "major" addresses and instead turned their focus to local constituencies and news outlets (Kernell [1986] 1997; Cohen 2008; Heith 2015). This going local strategy resulted in more domestic travel (Cook 2002) and a return to local rather than national audiences (Esbaugh-Soha and Peake 2006, 2011).

Another feature of this era was the rise of infotainment—a blend of news and entertainment. Ronald Reagan engaged primarily with traditional news outlets (cable was still in its infancy), but his appearance on *The Merv Griffin Show* presaged more regular presidential appearances on such venues (Gallagher 2017). George W. Bush made five such appearances, and Barack Obama fully embraced this entertainment-based strategy (Gallagher 2017, 23).

Information now comes not only from journalists and official sources but also from millions of citizens and other unofficial sources, including blogs and programs such as *The Daily Show, Colbert Report,* and *Saturday Night Live* (Williams and Delli Carpini 2011). Bloggers value being "out there" more than providing accurate information to the public (Elving 2013). This goal encourages punditry as opposed to the relaying of factual information. In addition, the media environment is defined by "an abundance of information but a lack of understanding of what it means" (Kumar 2010, 35) and by "outrage media coverage," which is "most easily recognizable by the rhetoric that defines it, with its hallmark venom, vilification of opponents, and hyperbolic reinterpretations of current events" (Sobieraj and Berry 2011, 2).

The combination of the twenty-four-hour news cycle; the proliferation of news sources, including the explosion of citizen-journalists; and the growth of outrage as a viable form of news coverage has left the American public misinformed and cynical. News organizations value being first to break the news, rather than being accurate. The media do little to help the public understand complicated issues of governance, and this can lead to misplaced blame, often on the president. Williams and Delli Carpini trace this new media environment to the 1990s and identify its six characteristics: (1) an increased volume of information; (2) an increased speed at which this information is gathered, retrieved, and transmitted; (3) an increase in consumer control; (4) fragmentation of audiences; (5) decentralization of certain aspects of media; and (6) greater interactive capacity between producers and consumers (2011, 1210).

An associated trend in the twenty-first century is polarization. Likely the result of a number of factors, including the growth of primaries, gerrymandering, and the personalization of politics, polarization is exacerbated by the discursive media environment and weak political parties. In combination, the fragmented media environment and increased polarization have shrunk the perusable public. Once again, it is very difficult for presidents to reach a truly national audience. Instead, they must reach out to targeted groups, often limited to their own partisans.

Targeting the Audience

During his attempt to pass health care reform, Bill Clinton (1993–2001) undertook a series of interviews to raise public awareness. This effort is directly comparable to the one taken by Barack Obama (2009–2017) years later. A comparison of the venues these two presidents used to promote their policies illustrates the changing media landscape.

In the approximately 126 interviews he gave between March and October 1993, Clinton addressed primarily regional media through traditional avenues (radio, TV, and newspaper). Table 6.1 shows a sample of these interviews. A couple of exceptions stand out: an interview with CNN's Larry King and MTV's Tabitha Soren.

Two decades later, Obama used a much wider array of media outlets in an attempt to reach all corners of a much more fragmented public (table 6.2). As a prime example, Obama appeared on Zach Galifianakis's *Between Two Ferns* in March 2014 to discuss health care and encourage enrollment in health insurance plans offered under the Affordable Care Act.[1] The audience of *Between Two Ferns* skews young and male— precisely the demographic that would likely be uninsured and unlikely to be reachable through more traditional venues (Dewey 2014). I call these audiences "targeted" because the president had a specific subgroup or demographic in mind. This interview eventually garnered more than fifty million views, dwarfing audiences for other presidential interviews or remarks (Elperin 2016). Obama also used traditional news networks, partisan outlets, and even appeared on Fox News a few times.

As table 6.3 shows, out of thirty-six selected interviews Obama gave on health care, more than half were to cable news or new media outlets (social media sites or programs available only through streaming services or websites). Obama also made an appearance on late-night TV and engaged with local media. A comparison of Clinton's and Obama's efforts on health care reveals the fragmentation of the media environment. Whereas Clinton addressed a majority of his interviews to regional

Table 6.1: Selected Bill Clinton Interviews on Health Care, 1993–1994[a]

Date	Interviewer	Media Type
March 13, 1993	Southern Florida media	Regional, traditional
March 13, 1993	California media	Regional, traditional
March 24, 1993	Dan Rather, CBS News	National, traditional
April 17, 1993	Mike Whitely, KDKA Radio, Pittsburgh	Regional, traditional
May 12, 1993	Don Imus, WFAN Radio, New York City	National, traditional
May 27, 1993	Connie Chung and Dan Rather, CBS News	National, traditional
June 21, 1993	Michael Jackson, KABC Radio, Los Angeles	Regional, traditional
June 21, 1993	Bob Levely, WMAL Radio, Washington, DC	Regional, traditional
July 14, 1993	Jan Mickelson, WHO Radio, Des Moines, IA	Regional, traditional
July 20, 1993	Wisconsin media	Regional, traditional
July 20, 1993	Louisiana media	Regional, traditional
July 20, 1993	Larry King, CNN	Targeted, cable TV
July 22, 1993	New York and New Jersey media	Regional, traditional
July 26, 1993	Indiana media, Chicago	Regional, traditional
July 27, 1993	Georgia media	Regional, traditional
July 28, 1993	Texas media	Regional, traditional
July 29, 1993	Nevada media	Regional, traditional
July 30, 1993	Arizona media	Regional, traditional
August 2, 1993	Newspaper editors	National, traditional
August 3, 1993	Nevada media	Regional, traditional
August 4, 1993	Louisiana media	Regional, traditional
September 21, 1993	Tabitha Soren, MTV	Targeted, cable TV
September 21, 1993	Radio talk-show hosts	National, traditional
October 18, 1993	Radio reporters	National, traditional
November 7, 1993	Timothy Russert and Tom Brokaw, *Meet the Press*	National, traditional
January 20, 1994	Larry King	National, cable TV
February 11, 1994	California newspaper publishers	Regional, traditional
February 17, 1994	Don Imus, WFAN Radio	National, traditional

April 19, 1994	MTV's Enough Is Enough Forum	Targeted, cable TV
May 3, 1994	CNN's Global Forum with President Clinton	Targeted
June 20, 1994	Katie Couric and Bryant Gumbel, *Today Show*	National, traditional
June 24, 1994	Kevin Horrigan and Charles Brennan, KMOX Radio, St. Louis	Regional, traditional
August 24, 1994	Gene Burns, WOR Radio, New York City	Regional, traditional
September 30, 1994	Alan Colmes	Targeted
October 12, 1994	Ellen Ratner	National
October 18, 1994	Mark Riley and Laura Blackburne, WLIB Radio, New York City	Regional
October 24, 1994	Chuck Meyer, WWWE Radio, Cleveland	Regional, traditional
October 31, 1994	Don Lancer, KYW Radio, Philadelphia	Regional, traditional
November 1, 1994	Bruce Newbury, WPRO Radio, Providence, RI l	Regional, traditiona
November 2, 1994	Ed Gordon, BET	Targeted

[a]From the American Presidency Project, using its categories.

radio and TV, Obama addressed a majority to targeted audiences. Obama mixed both partisan and cross-partisan media outlets.

Donald Trump gave fewer new media interviews than his predecessor. This strategy makes sense, given that the base of the Republican Party is older and less likely to be reached through these venues (Gallagher 2017). As table 6.4 shows, Trump also gave few interviews to traditional news outlets and focused on Fox News, a friendly, partisan outlet that Republicans watch closely. Absent from table 6.4 are Trump's frequent call-ins to Fox's morning news show (*Fox and Friends*) and Sean Hannity's evening program. Former CBS News White House correspondent Mark Knoller estimates that Trump gave sixty-one interviews to Fox, compared

Table 6.2: Selected Barack Obama Interviews on Health Care, 2009–2016[a]

Date	Interviewer	Media Type
February 3, 2009	Katie Couric, CBS News	National, traditional
September 20, 2009	David Gregory, *Meet the Press* (NBC)	National, traditional
December 13, 2009	Steve Kroft, *60 Minutes* (CBS)	National, traditional
December 23, 2009	*All Things Considered* (NPR)	National, traditional
December 23, 2009	Jim Lehrer, PBS	National, traditional
January 20, 2010	George Stephanopoulos, *Good Morning America* (ABC)	National, traditional
February 1, 2010	Steve Grove, YouTube	Targeted, new media[b]
March 17, 2010	Bret Baier, Fox News	Cross-partisan, cable news
March 29, 2010	Matt Lauer, *Today Show* (NBC)	National, traditional
April 21, 2010	John Harwood, CNBC	Targeted, cable news
June 3, 2010	Larry King, CNN	Targeted, cable news
July 15, 2010	Chuck Todd, *The Daily Rundown* (MSNBC)	Partisan, cable news
July 23, 2010	*Good Morning America* (ABC)	National, traditional
October 25, 2010	Eddie "Piolín" Sotelo, Univision Radio	Targeted, cable news
October 27, 2010	Jon Stewart, *The Daily Show* (Comedy Central)	Targeted, cable news
October 27, 2010	Michael Smerconish, MSNBC	Partisan, cable news
November 7, 2010	Steve Kroft, *60 Minutes* (CBS)	National, traditional
November 23, 2010	Barbara Walters, ABC (interview with Michelle Obama)	National, traditional
December 10, 2010	Steve Inskeep, NPR	National, traditional
April 18, 2011	David Crabtree, WRAL	Regional, traditional
July 22, 2011	Michel Martin, NPR	National, traditional
November 1, 2011	Mark Wilson, Fox 13–Tampa Bay	Regional, traditional
January 25, 2012	Maria Elena Salinas, Univision	Targeted, cable news

August 6, 2013	Jay Leno	National, late-night TV
December 5, 2013	Chris Mathews, *Hardball at American University* (MSNBC)	Partisan, cable news
February 2, 2014	Bill O'Reilly, Fox News	Cross-partisan, cable news
March 5, 2014	Jose Diaz-Balert and Enrique Acevedo, Univision News	Targeted, cable news
March 11, 2014	*Between Two Ferns*	Targeted, new media
August 2, 2014	*Economist* magazine	National, traditional
December 9, 2014	Jorge Ramos, Fusion and Univision News	Targeted, cable news
January 22, 2015	Steve Grove, director of News Lab at Google	Targeted, new media
February 15, 2015	Kara Swisher, Re/code, Stanford	Targeted, new media
June 22, 2015	Marc Maron	Targeted, new media
July 24, 2015	Jon Sopel, BBC	National, traditional
April 10, 2016	Chris Wallace, Fox News Sunday	Cross-partisan, cable news
May 9, 2016	*Daily Targum* (by phone)	Targeted, local
October 19, 2016	Ta-Nehisi Coates	Targeted, traditional

[a]From the American Presidency Project, using its categories.
[b]I use the term "new media" for any kind of social media, streaming service, or website.

with only seventeen to the traditional big-three networks (ABC, CBS, NBC) when these call-ins are included. By the end of his presidency, almost half of Trump's interviews were with Fox News (Kumar 2020).

This analysis illustrates an evolving approach from regional outlets to partisan ones. In some ways, Obama represents a bridge between these two approaches. Although he used a much more targeted approach than Clinton, he also incorporated cross-partisan outlets. Trump fully embraced the almost exclusive targeting of his own political base, similar to Polk's approach more than a century and a half ago. The depth of

Table 6.3: Health Care Interviews: Clinton vs. Obama[a]

Media Type	Clinton	Obama
National	11 of 41 (27%)	14 of 36 (39%)
Regional	22 of 41 (54%)	2 of 36 (5%)
Targeted	5 of 41 (12%)	20 of 36 (56%)

[a]Interview totals (41 for Clinton and 36 for Obama) include all interviews found in a search of the American Presidency Project using the parameter of speech-type interview and the keyword "healthcare."

polarization has made persuading the other side almost impossible, so presidents turn their efforts to motivating their own base of supporters.

The consequences of this targeted approach are clear. Given little opportunity and few incentives, presidents reach out to the public as a whole less and less often. Instead, they rely on communicating with their base and rallying their supporters. This strategy deepens partisan divisions and makes governing more difficult.

The Rise of Social Media and the Return of Written Communication

Beginning with George W. Bush (2001–2009) and accelerating through the presidencies of Barack Obama (2009–2017) and Donald Trump (2017–2021), presidents have revived the practice of communicating with the public in writing. The internet has allowed presidents to use Facebook, Twitter, Snapchat, and other means to reach the American people. Obama successfully used social media as a campaign tool to reach young people and minorities in 2008. While in office, Obama was dubbed the "first social media president," issuing the first tweet from the @POTUS account, answering questions on Facebook live, and using the first Snapchat filter (Bogost 2017).

Trump had more than eighty million followers on Twitter as of December 2020, which allowed him to circumvent the traditional media

Table 6.4: Selected Donald Trump Interviews, 2017–2020[a]

Date	Interviewer	Media Type
February 3, 2017	Bill O'Reilly, Fox News	Partisan, cable news
February 5, 2017	Jim Gray, Westwood One Sports Radio Network	Targeted, satellite radio
April 11, 2017	Maria Bartiromo, Fox Business Network	Partisan, cable news
April 21, 2017	Julie Pace, Associated Press White House correspondent	National, traditional
October 6, 2017	*Forbes* magazine editor Randall Lane and chief product officer Lewis D'Vorkin	Targeted, traditional
October 17, 2017	Mike Gallagher, Salem Radio Network	Local, traditional
October 17, 2017	Brian Kilmeade, Fox News Radio	Partisan, satellite radio
October 17, 2017	David Webb, Sirius XM Patriot Radio	Targeted, satellite radio
October 17, 2017	Tony Katz, WIBC Radio, Indianapolis	Local, traditional
October 17, 2017	Chris Plante, WMAL Radio, Washington, DC	Local, traditional
October 20, 2017	Maria Bartiromo, Fox Business Network	Partisan, cable TV
October 25, 2017	Lou Dobbs, Fox Business Network	Partisan, cable TV
January 11, 2018	*Wall Street Journal*	National, traditional
January 24, 2018	Reporters (subject: testifying under oath to special counsel Robert Mueller)	National, traditional
January 26, 2018	Joe Kernen, CNBC, at World Economic Forum in Davos, Switzerland	Targeted, cable TV
January 28, 2018	Piers Morgan, *Good Morning Britain*	Partisan, cable TV
October 14, 2018	Leslie Stahl, *60 Minutes* (CBS)	National, traditional
October 9, 2020	Rush Limbaugh, EIB Network	Targeted, radio

[a]From the American Presidency Project, using its categories. Known to be incomplete, as no all-inclusive list of Trump interviews exists at this point.

entirely before his account was suspended in January 2021.[2] As president, Trump used Twitter extensively, often tweeting many times per day.[3] He was the first president to use social media to enhance his personal connection with constituents (Kumar 2020). There is little doubt that Trump addressed much of his rhetoric on Twitter to his base (Stolee and Canton 2018). Although its effectiveness remains debatable, Trump's Twitter feed received as much attention as any single speech, if not more.

Of course, social media differs in important ways from written communications of the past. Twitter's limit on the number of characters encourages sound bites and other pithy responses. The visual aspect of social media allows users to share memes and videos, many of which are not in written form. At least in the case of Trump, the vetting of written presidential communications seems to have gone by the wayside. The nature of the internet allows immediate responses to news and events. Finally, social media allows individuals and institutions to have multiple accounts, amplifying their message. However, the larger point remains. Rather than responding to norms about how to communicate with the public, presidents react to the opportunities presented by technological innovation.

A Return to Normal?

It is too early to tell, but early signs suggest that the presidency of Joseph R. Biden (2021–) will return to more established patterns of communication. Biden utilizes Twitter, but in a much more traditional way than Trump, and much less frequently. For example, in the first week of May 2021, Biden sent five tweets from his @Joe Biden account: three expressed optimism about the future, one thanked Senators Ossof and Warnock and their supporters in Georgia, and one touted a promising jobs report. During the same period, Biden sent five additional tweets from the @POTUS account: commemorating Asian American, Native, Hawaii, and Pacific Islanders Month; thanking teachers on Teacher Appreciation Day; encouraging Americans to get vaccinated for COVID-19; detailing the American Rescue Plan; and encouraging Americans to tune in to Biden's remarks on the jobs report. It is too early to tell whether Biden's use of Twitter will be effective. With only slim majorities in Congress, his ability to get legislation passed relies on his ability to keep members of his own party on board with his policy priorities.

Biden has made more overtures to bipartisanship than Trump did. For example, though not specifically mentioning either party, Biden devoted six paragraphs of his January 20, 2021, inaugural address to the topic of unity. He used the word "unity" a total of nine times during the speech. In contrast, Trump's January 20, 2017, address mentioned unity only once, and it was in the context of a quote from the Bible. Trump did not attend Biden's inauguration, joining a small group of sitting presidents (John Adams, John Quincy Adams, and Andrew Johnson) who skipped their successors' swearing-in ceremonies. As history suggests, Biden's outreach to Republicans will be quite challenging in the current media environment and given the weakened state of political parties.[4] He is likely to be more successful in accomplishing his legislative goals if he can persuade and motivate his own supporters.

Conclusion

This work explains how American presidents have built relationships with the people of the United States. From George Washington traveling thirty miles a day on horseback to presidents today reaching tens of millions of followers on social media, a consistent desire for connection emerges. Beyond illuminating the history of popular presidential communication, this book clarifies how structural factors create incentives for political actors to change their behavior to gain an advantage. Since the inception of the republic, presidents have expended considerable time, energy, and effort in reaching the American public, signaling the centrality of this relationship to the democracy.

From Andrew Jackson's expert use of the administration newspaper to Franklin D. Roosevelt's brilliant use of the radio and Ronald Reagan's deep understanding of the importance of storytelling, these strategic choices added to these presidents' legacies.[1] Conversely, Andrew Johnson's inability to navigate a complicated media environment added to people's perception of his failures. Donald Trump's legacy remains to be seen, but his unique use of Twitter has led to reevaluations of social media strategies for politicians.

I have offered two heuristics for understanding and evaluating the evolution of popular presidential communication. The first is the persuadable public framework—that is, to whom the president is appealing and how much effort that persuasion will require. The second is the notion of opportunistic communication, which posits that presidents develop rhetorical strategies based on structural opportunities and an inherently competitive environment.

The Persuadable Public

Who constitutes the public and, perhaps more importantly, who the president can actually persuade have both changed considerably over time. The persuadable public is structured by factors outside of the president's control, including enfranchisement, the media environment, and the makeup of political parties. The persuadable public framework provides a useful tool for gauging both the purpose and the effectiveness of presidential rhetoric. The infrequent use of persuasion by the earliest presidents makes sense, given that the audience was small and reaching the people directly required considerable resources. The "going partisan" approach of mid-nineteenth-century presidents was strategic, based on the partisan media environment and travel limitations. By the late nineteenth century, presidents could be more ambitious in their persuasion efforts. Although newspapers remained partisan, the train allowed long-distance travel at unprecedented speed. Consequently, presidents could reach broad audiences directly. Presidents of the mid to late 1900s enjoyed a truly national audience created by radio and television and bolstered by the norm of journalistic objectivity. Given these circumstances, it is not surprising that some of these presidents, including Franklin D. Roosevelt, Lyndon Johnson, and Ronald Reagan, were viewed as exemplars in their efforts to go public. The rise of cable TV and the internet in the late twentieth century fractured the president's audience, and growing polarization made rhetorical leadership increasingly difficult.

In the twenty-first century, social media allow presidents to speak directly to the people without a middle man. The president can address a diversity of interests, microtargeting specific groups with tailored messages. However, this ability to speak directly to American citizens is mediated by a partisan press environment that colors and interprets the president's words. This practice is especially detrimental to the president's ability to reach across the aisle and therefore to govern effectively.

Moreover, the way presidents can reach the people has evolved, and technological innovation has made this outreach easier and less costly.

Accordingly, presidents have talked to the public more often as reaching them has become easier, again suggesting some utility to the exercise. Last, a president's own skills have created incentives for taking advantage of some of these new communication pathways. These same forces continue to shape presidential rhetoric in the twenty-first century. The use of four dimensions (mode, frequency, content, and audience) as analytical tools offers a dynamic approach to studying presidential rhetoric, allowing scholars to account for inevitable changes in technology, institutions, and political circumstances.

An important lesson of this evaluation of presidential rhetoric over time is that access to a national and truly persuadable audience, like the one presidents enjoyed in the mid-twentieth century, is an aberration. For most of American history, presidents have not had the luxury of a legitimately persuadable public. Instead, a partisan media environment, though taking different forms, has made it difficult for presidents to reach opponents in the public sphere. The recentness of this unique period in presidential rhetorical history, and the tendency to focus on presidents in this era, has resulted in unrealistic expectations of the purpose and effect of popular presidential communication.

Opportunistic Communication

Throughout this book, I have shown that rather than responding to some universally understood norm about the appropriateness of public outreach, presidents have responded to the opportunities presented to them. For most of American history, presidents have had to contend with an imperfect environment that made it difficult for them to reach the public as a whole. The incentives to use a "going public" strategy when the ability to reach the people is highly constrained are limited. It makes more sense to expend resources on other activities, including motivating supporters or disciplining fellow party members.

With this in mind, the future of presidential communication strategies will continue to depend on the technologies available and the nature of the media environment. As history has shown, it usually takes some time for politicians to figure out how to best utilize new and emerging technologies. Whether Trump's use of social media represents a mastery of the technology is yet to be seen. Of course, we can only speculate about what the next innovation will be and how it might influence presidential communication strategies. However, we should expect presidents to continue to find new ways to reach their intended audiences.

To take advantage of new opportunities, politicians have to solve problems, including how to get and hold people's attention. So as the media landscape grows more complex, politics becomes more about performance and entertainment than policy and substance. Scholars are mistaken when they draw arbitrary lines rather than viewing these changes as the natural evolution of a complex institution embedded in a competitive political environment.

By looking across time and charting the development of the institution of the presidency, the larger story of American political development becomes more fully fleshed out. In the increased frequency of presidential rhetoric, we can see the enhanced importance of the presidency. The expanded role of the president and, by extension, the public in the policymaking process is illuminated by a focus on the content of presidential rhetoric. Consideration of the persuadable public helps elucidate presidents' motives behind their communication strategies. This analysis makes it clear that presidents are intimately connected to the American public and that they can facilitate the people's participation in politics. At the same time, even in the earliest days of the republic, presidents relied on the public for support. The very essence of American politics is built on this complex but enduring reciprocal relationship.

Appendix

Data for Inaugural Addresses and Annual Messages[a]

President	Year	Flesch Reading Ease	Lag Flesch	Grade Level	Words	Year_Count	Tulis	Inaugural
Washington	1789	28.3	NA	17.5	1089	0	0	0
Washington	1789	19.7	28.3	21.8	1428	0	0	1
Washington	1790	33.6	19.7	17.5	1401	1	0	0
Washington	1791	27.2	33.6	18.2	2302	2	0	0
Washington	1792	32.6	27.2	17	2101	3	0	0
Washington	1793	38.3	32.6	15.6	1968	4	0	0
Washington	1793	34.4	38.3	16.7	135	4	0	1
Washington	1794	35.7	34.4	15.8	2918	5	0	0
Washington	1795	26.9	35.7	18.3	1989	6	0	0
Washington	1796	31.6	26.9	17.2	2871	7	0	0
Adams, J.	1797	32.6	31.6	17.2	2063	8	0	0
Adams, J.	1797	22.9	32.6	20.5	2319	8	0	1
Adams, J.	1798	30.5	22.9	18	2218	9	0	0
Adams, J.	1799	25.5	30.5	18.8	1505	10	0	0
Adams, J.	1800	33.2	25.5	16.3	1372	11	0	0
Jefferson	1801	36.3	33.2	16.1	3224	12	0	0
Jefferson	1801	47.8	36.3	13.2	1721	12	0	1
Jefferson	1802	40.2	47.8	15.6	2197	13	0	0
Jefferson	1803	24.6	40.2	19.8	2263	14	0	0
Jefferson	1804	32.8	24.6	17.6	2096	15	0	0
Jefferson	1805	38.5	32.8	16.7	2927	16	0	0
Jefferson	1805	41.8	38.5	14.9	2158	16	0	1
Jefferson	1806	35.8	41.8	16.7	2860	17	0	0

(continued on the next page)

President	Year	Flesch Reading Ease	Lag Flesch	Grade Level	Words	Year_Count	Tulis	Inaugural
Jefferson	1807	35.4	35.8	16.9	2384	18	0	0
Jefferson	1808	31.3	35.4	17.8	2675	19	0	0
Madison	1809	22.7	31.3	20.6	1831	20	0	0
Madison	1809	36.1	22.7	16	1173	20	0	1
Madison	1810	22.4	36.1	20	2446	21	0	0
Madison	1811	22.1	22.4	20.7	2273	22	0	0
Madison	1812	31.1	22.1	17.5	3242	23	0	0
Madison	1813	25.1	31.1	20.2	3257	24	0	0
Madison	1813	39.1	25.1	15.5	1210	24	0	1
Madison	1814	27.5	39.1	19.4	2111	25	0	0
Madison	1815	18.7	27.5	21	3146	26	0	0
Madison	1816	24.3	18.7	19.7	3364	27	0	0
Monroe	1817	35.5	24.3	16.5	4418	28	0	0
Monroe	1817	45	35.5	13.1	3367	29	0	1
Monroe	1818	31.4	45	17.6	4376	30	0	0
Monroe	1819	37.2	31.4	16.2	4702	31	0	0
Monroe	1820	32	37.2	17.8	3438	32	0	0
Monroe	1821	32.8	32	17.8	5814	33	0	0
Monroe	1821	39.5	32.8	15.6	4461	33	0	1
Monroe	1822	30.9	39.5	17.9	4720	34	0	0
Monroe	1823	33.4	30.9	16.6	6354	35	0	0
Monroe	1824	37.6	33.4	16	8399	36	0	0
Adams, J. Q.	1825	25.7	37.6	18.9	8974	37	0	0
Adams, J. Q.	1825	37.2	25.7	14.5	2907	37	0	1
Adams, J. Q.	1826	22	37.2	19.8	7706	38	0	0
Adams, J. Q.	1827	20.2	22	19.9	6913	39	0	0
Adams, J. Q.	1828	28.4	20.2	17.4	7280	40	0	0
Jackson	1829	33	28.4	16.8	10521	41	0	0
Jackson	1829	24.4	33	19.8	1124	41	0	1
Jackson	1830	30.6	24.4	17.8	15090	42	0	0
Jackson	1831	28.8	30.6	18.8	7177	43	0	0
Jackson	1832	29.4	28.8	18.4	7863	44	0	0
Jackson	1833	25.8	29.4	19.9	7876	45	0	0
Jackson	1833	33	24.6	16.4	1171	46	0	1
Jackson	1834	24.6	25.8	19.8	13404	46	0	0

Jackson	1834	25.1	33	20.1	10825	47	0	0
Jackson	1835	28.3	25.1	19	12364	48	0	0
Van Buren	1836	29	28.3	18.1	11434	49	0	0
Van Buren	1837	26.1	29	18.7	11474	50	0	0
Van Buren	1838	32.4	26.1	17.3	13416	51	0	0
Van Buren	1839	34.8	32.4	15.5	3826	51	0	1
Van Buren	1840	20.3	34.8	20.6	8975	52	0	0
Harrison, W. H.	1841	32.1	27.8	17.8	8425	56	0	1
Tyler	1841	27.1	20.3	19.2	8241	53	0	0
Tyler	1842	29.2	27.1	18.5	8403	54	0	0
Tyler	1843	27.8	29.2	18.9	8025	55	0	0
Tyler	1844	33.6	32.1	16.8	9311	57	0	0
Polk	1845	31	33.6	17.6	16112	58	0	0
Polk	1845	35.8	31	15.6	4798	58	0	1
Polk	1846	30.5	35.8	17.8	18222	59	0	0
Polk	1847	31	30.5	17.7	16407	60	0	0
Polk	1848	31	31	17.3	21288	61	0	0
Taylor	1849	28.5	31	17.8	7617	62	0	0
Taylor	1849	24.5	28.5	19.4	1087	62	0	1
Fillmore	1850	32.5	24.5	16.9	8318	63	0	0
Fillmore	1851	28	32.5	18.3	13244	64	0	0
Fillmore	1852	34	28	16.4	9923	65	0	0
Pierce	1853	24.5	34	19.2	9586	66	0	0
Pierce	1853	37.7	24.5	15.3	3329	66	0	1
Pierce	1854	28.7	37.7	17.4	10134	67	0	0
Pierce	1855	24.1	28.7	19.4	11610	68	0	0
Pierce	1856	25.6	24.1	18.4	10473	69	0	0
Buchanan	1857	31.7	25.6	16.7	13651	70	0	0
Buchanan	1857	37.2	31.7	15.8	2820	70	0	1
Buchanan	1858	32.5	37.2	16.3	16347	71	0	0
Buchanan	1859	33.2	32.5	16.5	12337	72	0	0
Buchanan	1860	36.5	33.2	15	14028	73	0	0
Lincoln	1861	36.2	36.5	15.6	6976	74	0	0
Lincoln	1861	47.1	36.2	12.6	3628	74	0	1
Lincoln	1862	43.1	47.1	12.9	8367	75	0	0
Lincoln	1863	30.9	43.1	16.4	6112	76	0	0
Lincoln	1864	33.2	30.9	15.2	5863	77	0	0
Lincoln	1865	59.3	40.5	11.1	693	78	0	1

(continued on the next page)

Appendix

President	Year	Flesch Reading Ease	Lag Flesch	Grade Level	Words	Year_Count	Tulis	Inaugural
Johnson, A.	1865	40.5	33.2	14.5	9220	78	0	0
Johnson, A.	1866	25.6	59.3	17.6	7129	79	0	0
Johnson, A.	1867	36.9	25.6	15	11997	80	0	0
Johnson, A.	1868	26.6	36.9	16.7	9821	81	0	0
Grant	1869	37.8	26.6	14.8	7689	82	0	0
Grant	1869	46.3	37.8	13	1121	82	0	1
Grant	1870	35.7	46.3	15.6	8734	83	0	0
Grant	1871	35.5	35.7	15.7	6455	84	0	0
Grant	1872	30.4	35.5	16.3	10093	85	0	0
Grant	1873	31.8	30.4	16.5	10022	86	0	0
Grant	1873	48	31.8	13.1	1335	86	0	1
Grant	1874	35.7	48	16.1	9791	87	0	0
Grant	1875	33	35.7	16.5	12200	88	0	0
Grant	1876	29.2	33	17.6	6791	89	0	0
Hayes	1877	26.8	29.2	18.1	10723	90	0	0
Hayes	1877	29.3	26.8	18.1	2471	90	0	1
Hayes	1878	24	29.3	18	7879	91	0	0
Hayes	1879	23.4	24	18.7	11634	92	0	0
Hayes	1880	28.8	23.4	16.8	13345	93	0	0
Garfield	1881	43.5	30.7	13.5	2973	94	0	1
Arthur	1881	30.7	28.8	16	13324	94	0	0
Arthur	1882	32	43.5	16.5	10273	95	0	0
Arthur	1883	31.2	32	16.2	8364	96	0	0
Arthur	1884	30.6	31.2	16.2	8917	97	0	0
Cleveland	1885	28.9	30.6	17.1	19748	98	0	0
Cleveland	1885	32.2	28.9	17	1682	98	0	1
Cleveland	1886	25.2	32.2	18.1	15135	99	0	0
Cleveland	1887	27.8	25.2	18.4	5290	100	0	0
Cleveland	1888	25.6	27.8	17.4	13222	101	0	0
Harrison, B.	1889	34.6	25.6	15.7	13004	102	0	0
Harrison, B.	1889	40.1	34.6	14.3	4385	102	0	1
Harrison, B.	1890	32.7	40.1	16.1	11522	103	0	0
Harrison, B.	1891	31.2	32.7	17.1	16306	104	0	0
Harrison, B.	1892	26.7	31.2	17.2	13680	105	0	0
Cleveland	1893	19.1	26.7	18.4	12282	106	0	0

Cleveland	1893	29.5	19.1	17.4	2013	106	0	1
Cleveland	1894	21.3	29.5	18.4	15892	107	0	0
Cleveland	1895	21.6	21.3	19.8	14670	108	0	0
Cleveland	1896	22.5	21.6	18.8	15453	109	0	0
McKinley	1897	32.7	22.5	16.3	12113	110	0	0
McKinley	1897	38.2	32.7	14.9	3957	110	0	1
McKinley	1898	25.8	38.2	17.7	20224	111	0	0
McKinley	1899	28.8	25.8	16.8	19142	112	0	0
McKinley	1900	27.1	28.8	16.8	19142	113	0	0
McKinley	1901	43.6	44.1	12.5	2215	114	0	1
Roosevelt, T.	1901	44.1	27.1	13.2	19588	114	0	0
Roosevelt, T.	1902	43.6	43.6	13.5	9782	115	0	0
Roosevelt, T.	1903	37.4	43.6	14.4	14932	116	0	0
Roosevelt, T.	1904	39.8	37.4	14.7	17406	117	0	0
Roosevelt, T.	1905	41.6	39.8	14.3	25033	118	0	0
Roosevelt, T.	1905	55.3	41.6	11.7	983	118	0	1
Roosevelt, T.	1906	42.2	55.3	14.3	23575	119	0	0
Roosevelt, T.	1907	41.4	42.2	14.3	27381	120	0	0
Roosevelt, T.	1908	41.5	41.4	14	19378	121	0	0
Taft	1909	25.6	41.5	18.3	13889	122	0	0
Taft	1909	34.9	25.6	16.4	5427	122	0	1
Taft	1910	31.6	34.9	16.6	27568	123	0	0
Taft	1911	31.6	31.6	16.4	23739	124	0	0
Taft	1912	28.8	31.6	17.3	25163	125	0	0
Wilson	1913	45.5	28.8	13.9	3553	126	0	0
Wilson	1913	60.1	45.5	10.2	1699	126	0	1
Wilson	1914	59.1	60.1	10.6	4540	127	1	0
Wilson	1915	42.3	59.1	14.6	7692	128	1	0
Wilson	1916	32.2	42.3	16.9	2117	129	1	0
Wilson	1917	53.8	32.2	12.1	3921	130	1	0
Wilson	1917	62.4	53.8	10.1	1522	130	1	1
Wilson	1918	46	62.4	14	5471	131	1	0
Wilson	1919	39.8	46	14.4	4756	132	1	0
Wilson	1920	32.1	39.8	17.1	2708	133	1	0
Harding	1921	35.3	32.1	14.7	5603	134	1	0
Harding	1921	44.3	35.3	12.1	3323	134	1	1
Harding	1922	37.8	44.3	14	5745	135	1	0
Coolidge	1923	45.4	37.8	11.2	6702	136	1	0

(continued on the next page)

President	Year	Flesch Reading Ease	Lag Flesch	Grade Level	Words	Year_ Count	Tulis	Inaugural
Coolidge	1924	36.7	45.4	14.2	6964	137	1	0
Coolidge	1925	39.8	36.7	13	10848	138	1	0
Coolidge	1925	50.9	39.8	11.1	4055	138	1	1
Coolidge	1926	39.9	50.9	13.2	10313	139	1	0
Coolidge	1927	41.8	39.9	12.1	8777	140	1	0
Coolidge	1928	38.4	41.8	13	8066	141	1	0
Hoover	1929	30.9	38.4	14.9	10990	142	1	0
Hoover	1929	43.8	30.9	11.9	3837	142	1	1
Hoover	1930	27.9	43.8	14.9	4533	143	1	0
Hoover	1931	31.4	27.9	14.1	5680	144	1	0
Hoover	1932	33.4	31.4	14.5	4207	145	1	0
Roosevelt, F. D.	1933	55.7	33.4	10.1	1880	146	1	1
Roosevelt, F. D.	1934	40	55.7	14.3	2226	147	1	0
Roosevelt, F. D.	1935	43.6	40	12.9	3525	148	1	0
Roosevelt, F. D.	1936	52.6	43.6	11.2	3820	149	1	0
Roosevelt, F. D.	1937	39.5	52.6	13.8	2732	150	1	0
Roosevelt, F. D.	1937	56.3	39.5	9.5	1807	150	1	1
Roosevelt, F. D.	1938	44.3	56.3	13	4697	151	1	0
Roosevelt, F. D.	1939	48.3	44.3	11.7	3765	152	1	0
Roosevelt, F. D.	1940	48.7	48.3	12.7	3198	153	1	0
Roosevelt, F. D.	1941	52.1	48.7	11.1	3312	154	1	0
Roosevelt, F. D.	1941	61.9	52.1	9.2	1354	154	1	1
Roosevelt, F. D.	1942	59.1	61.9	9.6	3506	155	1	0
Roosevelt, F. D.	1943	54.7	59.1	11	4588	156	1	0
Roosevelt, F. D.	1944	52.9	54.7	11.1	3805	157	1	0
Roosevelt, F. D.	1945	45.9	52.9	12.5	8211	158	1	0
Roosevelt, F. D.	1945	70.7	45.9	8	556	158	1	1
Truman	1946	34.5	70.7	13.7	27678	159	1	0
Truman	1947	42.2	34.5	12.2	6047	160	1	0
Truman	1948	50.4	42.2	10.7	5087	161	1	0
Truman	1949	48.2	50.4	10.9	3397	162	1	0
Truman	1949	50.8	48.2	10.9	2263	162	1	1
Truman	1950	49.2	50.8	11.6	5126	163	1	0
Truman	1951	62.2	49.2	8.6	3989	164	1	0
Truman	1952	62.8	62.2	8.9	5336	165	1	0

Truman	1953	52.3	62.8	11.1	9602	166	1	0
Eisenhower	1953	60.4	52.3	9.6	2445	166	1	1
Eisenhower	1954	40.1	60.4	12.3	6942	167	1	0
Eisenhower	1955	39.2	40.1	12.5	5973	168	1	0
Eisenhower	1956	36.2	39.2	13	7234	169	1	0
Eisenhower	1957	38.7	36.2	12.8	8248	170	1	0
Eisenhower	1957	70.3	38.7	7.6	1636	170	1	1
Eisenhower	1958	45.2	70.3	11.6	4910	171	1	0
Eisenhower	1959	45.7	45.2	11.4	4947	172	1	0
Eisenhower	1960	41.6	45.7	12.6	5628	173	1	0
Eisenhower	1961	30.8	41.6	13.9	6192	174	1	0
Kennedy	1961	42.2	30.8	13.2	5170	175	1	0
Kennedy	1961	58.2	42.2	11.4	1339	175	1	1
Kennedy	1962	44.6	58.2	12.5	6441	176	1	0
Kennedy	1963	48.6	44.6	11.9	5327	177	1	0
Johnson, L. B.	1964	51.3	48.6	11.2	3190	178	1	0
Johnson, L. B.	1965	61.1	51.3	8.6	4406	179	1	0
Johnson, L. B.	1965	71.6	61.1	7	1495	179	1	1
Johnson, L. B.	1966	55.3	71.6	10.7	5496	180	1	0
Johnson, L. B.	1967	54.8	55.3	10.3	7112	181	1	0
Johnson, L. B.	1968	53.4	54.8	10.3	4861	182	1	0
Johnson, L. B.	1969	55.4	53.4	10.7	4099	183	1	0
Nixon	1969	70.5	55.4	7.7	2105	183	1	1
Nixon	1970	54	70.5	11	4462	184	1	0
Nixon	1971	53.5	54	11.6	4486	185	1	0
Nixon	1972	53.1	53.5	11.1	3968	186	1	0
Nixon	1973	43.9	53.1	13.7	1649	187	1	0
Nixon	1973	57.3	43.9	11.4	1793	187	1	1
Nixon	1974	50.4	57.3	12.4	5175	188	1	0
Ford	1975	45.8	50.4	11	4117	189	1	0
Ford	1976	49.3	45.8	10.7	4953	190	1	0
Ford	1977	45.2	49.3	11.9	4712	191	1	0
Carter	1977	59	45.2	9.9	1215	191	1	1
Carter	1978	55.8	59	9.9	4590	192	1	0
Carter	1978	33	55.8	13.5	12090	192	1	0
Carter	1979	49.8	33	11.2	3276	193	1	0
Carter	1979	31.8	49.8	14.2	21477	193	1	0
Carter	1980	50	31.8	11.2	3469	194	1	0

(continued on the next page)

President	Year	Flesch Reading Ease	Lag Flesch	Grade Level	Words	Year_Count	Tulis	*Inaugural*
Carter	1980	31.5	50	14.2	33896	194	1	0
Carter	1981	29.9	31.5	14.6	33740	195	1	0
Reagan	1981	48.2	29.9	11.3	4450	196	1	0
Reagan	1981	62.3	48.2	9	2423	196	1	1
Reagan	1982	51.3	62.3	10.9	5182	197	1	0
Reagan	1983	49.9	51.3	11.3	5565	198	1	0
Reagan	1984	56	49.9	9.3	4956	199	1	0
Reagan	1985	55.6	56	9.7	4229	200	1	0
Reagan	1985	61.1	55.6	9.3	2571	200	1	1
Reagan	1986	57.7	61.1	9.7	3484	201	1	0
Reagan	1987	56.9	57.7	9.8	3801	202	1	0
Reagan	1988	52.6	56.9	11	4864	203	1	0
Bush, G. H. W.	1989	61.8	52.6	8.4	4805	204	1	0
Bush, G. H. W.	1989	77.4	61.8	6	2341	204	1	1
Bush, G. H. W.	1990	60.9	77.4	9.1	3771	205	1	0
Bush, G. H. W.	1991	57.1	60.9	9.2	3943	206	1	0
Bush, G. H. W.	1992	68.5	57.1	7.5	5084	207	1	0
Clinton	1993	56.8	68.5	10.9	7007	208	1	0
Clinton	1993	63.1	56.8	8.3	1598	208	1	1
Clinton	1994	62.3	63.1	9	7397	209	1	0
Clinton	1995	62.6	62.3	9.3	9198	210	1	0
Clinton	1996	59	62.6	9.3	6336	211	1	0
Clinton	1997	58.3	59	9.6	6762	212	1	0
Clinton	1997	61.3	58.3	9.5	2156	212	1	1
Clinton	1998	57.4	61.3	9.7	7321	213	1	0
Clinton	1999	55.8	57.4	10	7497	214	1	0
Clinton	2000	59.3	55.8	9.3	9087	215	1	0
Bush, G. W.	2001	59.9	59.3	8.6	4365	216	1	0
Bush, G. W.	2001	62.9	59.9	8.3	1582	216	1	1
Bush, G. W.	2002	57.3	62.9	9.3	3825	217	1	0
Bush, G. W.	2003	51.9	57.3	10.4	5374	218	1	0
Bush, G. W.	2004	54.3	51.9	10.2	5172	219	1	0
Bush, G. W.	2005	48.3	54.3	11.3	5053	220	1	0
Bush, G. W.	2005	56.8	48.3	10.3	2071	220	1	1
Bush, G. W.	2006	50.6	56.8	10.8	5305	221	1	0

Bush, G. W.	2007	57	50.6	9.8	5549	222	1	0
Bush, G. W.	2008	54.6	57	10	5807	223	1	0
Obama	2009	59	54.6	10	5902	224	1	0
Obama	2009	66.2	59	8.5	2389	224	1	1
Obama	2010	60.6	66.2	9	7229	225	1	0
Obama	2011	62.9	60.6	8.7	6869	226	1	0
Obama	2012	60.9	62.9	8.8	7018	227	1	0
Obama	2013	58.8	60.9	9.5	6808	228	1	0
Obama	2013	61.6	62.9	9.5	2103	229	1	1
Obama	2014	58.5	60.9	9.6	7013	230	1	0
Obama	2015	61.9	58.5	9	6764	231	1	0
Obama	2016	64.8	61.9	8.2	6061	232	1	0
Trump	2017	62.3	64.8	8.3	1458	233	1	1
Trump	2017	58.7	62.3	9.2	5020	233	1	0
Trump	2018	59.7	58.7	8.6	5851	234	1	0
Trump	2019	57.5	59.7	8.8	5577	235	1	0
Trump	2020	53.0	57.5	9.6	6326	236	1	0

[a]Variable values for linear regression.

Notes

Introduction

1. Historically, enfranchisement is an important aspect of audience.

2. I touch briefly on Joseph R. Biden, but given the newness of the administration, an in-depth analysis is not possible at this time.

3. Citations to *The Rhetorical Presidency* exceed sixteen hundred; more than three hundred of these citations have appeared since 2017, many of them in textbooks, and are essentially unchallenged. These numbers illustrate the continued dominance of Tulis's account, despite excellent rebuttals.

4. Many of these remarks are not cataloged in the Richardson Papers: A Compilation of Messages and Papers of the Presidents 1787–1902 or the American Presidency Project, although I have shared these discoveries with the latter.

5. The American Presidency Project provides the text of all inaugural addresses, annual messages, and State of the Union addresses and is my source for these text throughout the book.

6. Clearly, deliberation on its own is not necessarily a cure-all, given that lawmakers in the nineteenth century were unable to resolve the most significant crisis the nation ever faced, and that resolution occurred only through succession and civil war.

7. Other scholars with a similar approach include Hoffman (2002), Campbell and Jamieson (2008), Laracey (2002, 2008), Medhurst (2008), Ellis (1998), and Stuckey (1991).

8. These keywords included *president*, the president's last name, *speech, response, reply, tour*, and *trip*.

9. I accessed the early collections through the University of California–Santa Barbara Library website. The *New York Times, Washington Post, San Francisco Chronicle, Los Angeles Times*, and *Chicago Tribune* are available through the ProQuest Historical Newspaper database.

10. More broadly, Jeffrey Pasley (2001) shows that newspapers were central to American politics in the early republic.

Chapter 1. Going Elite: George Washington to
John Q. Adams, 1789–1828

1. The Society of the Cincinnati is the nation's oldest patriotic organization, founded in 1783 by officers of the Continental army and their French counterparts who served together in the American Revolution (www.societyofthecin cinnati.org).

2. Many excellent scholarly books have been written about the Constitutional Convention and the debates that took place there. My goal is not to rehash these debates in detail. Instead, I offer an accessible overview of scholarly opinions on the convention, with a focus on the presidency.

3. I include John Quincy Adams as part of the founding generation because of his intellectual proximity to many of the most influential political thinkers of the time, including his father.

4. The Jay Treaty attempted to resolve some of the remaining issues between the United States and Great Britain. However, many critics found aspects of the treaty humiliating to the United States and resisted its approval (https://www.sen ate.gov/about/powers-procedures/treaties/uproar-over-senate-treaty-approval .htm).

5. The custom during the Washington and Adams administrations was that after the president delivered his annual message to Congress, the Senate and House each issued a reply to the president's statement. Members of Congress would then go to the White House to hear the president's response to their statements.

6. The XYZ affair was a diplomatic incident between France and the United States. President Adams sent ministers to France in an effort to secure US shipping, and while in France, these ministers were offered a bribe. In the spring of 1798 correspondence among these officials was made public, and the American public was outraged. The incident was peacefully settled in the Convention of 1800 (Stinchcombe 1980).

7. A search of nineteenth-century newspapers returns thousands of hits for presidents' annual messages. Articles were published in anticipation of the message, the entire message itself was reprinted, and editorial reactions to the message appeared for days and sometimes weeks after it was delivered to Congress.

8. Lyon had a unique background. Before being elected to the House in 1796, he was a printer and indentured servant. His humble roots and his career as a newspaperman led the Federalists in Congress to treat him badly, mocking "his ethnicity and accent during House debates" (Pasley 2001, 110). Once in Congress,

one of the first practices Lyon criticized was the "aristocratic custom of replying to the presidential message," and the new congressman requested to be excused from attending the reply (Purcell 1936, 55).

Chapter 2. Going Partisan: Andrew Jackson to Abraham Lincoln, 1829–1865

1. Important innovations in the mid-1800s allowed the newspaper to be distributed over greater distances and with more speed and accuracy. The technological advances that directly affected the newspaper industry included electricity, the telegraph, the mechanical press, the four-cylinder machine, Linotype and Monotype, and the typewriter (Gramling 1940; Tebbel 1969; Cornwell 1979).

2. According to the US Census, the population of the United States was roughly seven million in 1810 and ten million in 1830.

3. A search of American's Historical Newspapers Database using the keywords "Jackson," "president," and "bank" for 1832–1836 returns more than 1,660 results. Importantly, this is only a fraction of the newspapers publishing during this period.

4. Calhoun had been Jackson's first vice president and considered running against him in 1832 (Meacham 2008).

5. The *Madisonian* became Tyler's newspaper during the veto battle. The paper was only a year old in 1842, making it somewhat weak and not as effective as the president would have liked (Pollard 1947).

6. The letter, as reprinted in the *Ohio Democrat*, was simply dated November 1841. However, the letter appeared in the paper on November 25, 1841.

7. Korzi (2004) distinguishes this strategy from "going public" because the president's audience was only his partisans instead of the nation.

8. The *Daily Union* (Washington, DC) can be searched at https://chroniclin gamerica.loc.gov/lccn/sn82003410/.

9. Whether Jackson (or any president) actually had a mandate is a different question that I do not examine here. See Azari (2014) for a discussion of presidential mandates.

Chapter 3. Going Regional: Andrew Johnson to Benjamin Harrison, 1866–1893

1. The railroad is the most important innovation influencing presidential rhetoric. However, it can also be viewed as a proxy for the broader technological

shift the country was undergoing, which likely had an effect on the president's ability to communicate more efficiently with the public.

2. Other inventions include the telegraph (1830s–1840s), typewriter (1868), telephone (1876), and electric light (1879).

3. Peak railroad mileage was reached in 1916 (Stover 2008).

4. I use 300,300 as the peak number of railroad miles and divide the number of railroad miles completed by 300,300 to arrive at a percentage for the year.

5. Others, including Ellis (2008, 90–97) and Pollard (1947), discuss Johnson's tour in detail, but it merits coverage here for two reasons: (1) As stated, Johnson represents the first significant increase in popular presidential communication, so the opportunities he sought to communicate should be investigated—given that these opportunities are central to my claims about the causes behind the development of presidential rhetoric. (2) Tulis (1987) argues that Johnson's willingness to talk about policy with the public was one of the reasons for his impeachment. Tulis's claim that Johnson was an aberration in presidential rhetoric rather than an example of a natural development given new opportunities continues to have purchase.

6. Some of these hits include multiple articles.

7. One problem with this sample is that the *New York Times* was supportive of Johnson, suggesting that I would have a higher percentage of supportive articles. However, I should still be able to detect a shift in tone, and this approach allows me to illustrate an alternative narrative to the one adopted by many scholars.

8. Presidents had been touring since George Washington, so the tour itself was not innovative.

9. My interpretation of the evidence in historical newspapers is supported by Phifer (1952).

10. These interviews were widely copied or commented on by other newspapers (Pollard 1947).

11. In the 1876 election, Hayes lost the popular vote to his opponent Samuel Tilden. Votes in the Electoral College were tied, with four states submitting competing slates of electors. In an effort to resolve these inconsistencies, Congress created a fifteen-person commission, and after months of deliberation, it ruled along partisan lines and declared that Hayes was president. To get the Democrats to accept the commission's decision, the Republicans agreed to withdraw federal troops from Florida, South Carolina, and Louisiana. Hayes faced threats of assassination and the prospect of a congressional filibuster to prevent his inauguration (Vazzano 2006).

12. Arthur provided little leadership through his written communications. Of

his 463 written messages, 405 were special messages that accompanied reports, responses to congressional inquiries, and other mundane business that did nothing to advance the president's legislative priorities. Another fifty were proclamations and executive orders of a ceremonial nature, including recognition of holidays and exhibition openings. Arthur's eight remaining written communications were four annual messages and four vetoes, including a veto of the Chinese Exclusion Act, which angered labor, and a veto of the River and Harbor Act, which was overridden by Congress the next day (presidency.ucsb.org; https://millercenter .org/president/chester-arthur/key-events).

13. I discuss Cleveland in both this chapter and the following one because he served two nonconsecutive terms. During his second term, his approach to tariff legislation was an important precursor to Woodrow Wilson's.

14. Although I have not systematically coded these data, this was yet another way the president could communicate with the public, despite persistent limitations.

15. Again, this example illustrates the fluidity of my categories. Harrison toured the nation but still spoke to small audiences. This was inevitable until the invention of the radio, which allowed presidents to address the whole country.

Chapter 4. Going Almost National: Grover Cleveland
to Woodrow Wilson, 1894–1921

1. Written rhetoric became even more important for Cleveland in 1894, when he had surgery to remove a tumor from his mouth. This included the removal of "five teeth, about a third of the upper palate, and a large piece of the upper left jawbone" (Algeo 2011, 92). Cleveland was fitted for a prosthetic jaw, which made speaking difficult (Algeo 2011).

2. There is no single definition of the powers of the presidency, partly because the founders created a vague institution open to interpretation, leading to competing visions about the nature of the president and his role in government. However, these interpretations do not necessarily rise to the level of a norm.

3. The American Tract Society was the first US organization to publish and distribute the printed word on a mass scale (Tompkins 1985, 150).

4. I was unable to locate all 350 of Taft's speeches. I found about 100 speeches using my keyword search methodology of historical newspapers. This suggests that my data represent an *undercount* of presidential speech. These results are not surprising given that I was searching a limited number of newspapers and that reporting around speeches on tour was often confusing and non-comprehensive.

5. See Laracey (2021) for an in-depth treatment of Jefferson's decision to deliver the annual message in writing.

6. The Flesch score (from 0 to 100) was developed in 1948 by psychologist R. Flesch. The higher the score, the more readable the passage. The Flesch score is calculated using the following formula: $206.835 - (1.015 \times ASL) - (84.6 \times ASW)$, where ASL is the average sentence length and ASW is the average word length.

7. For information about the segmentation function, see http://cran.r-project .org/web/packages/segme'nted/segmented.pdf.

8. I used year_count = 125 (equivalent to 1913) for the value of psi (the estimated break point).

9. There may be other interpretations of Wilson's action that I have overlooked. However, although my sample is not entirely random, it is not systematically biased toward my hypothesis. It includes two "national" newspapers (*New York Times* and *Washington Post*) and numerous local ones.

10. The paper incorrectly printed "Lyons" instead of "Lyon."

11. Matthew Lyon represented two states: Vermont and Kentucky. He was the second member of Congress to do so. Lyon was imprisoned for violating the Sedition Acts when he accused President Adams of "an unbounded thirst for ridiculous pomp." See http://history.house.gov/HistoricalHighlight/Detail/36323.

12. I found corroboration that Lyon also denounced the custom of replying to the president's message and asked to be excused from that presentation. Although I could find only one source that mentioned Jefferson making any promises to Lyon (Purcell 1936), it is worth noting that Lyon cast the deciding vote for Jefferson in the 1800 election, so he may have had some sway over the president.

13. This letter was addressed to the president of the Senate and accompanied Jefferson's first annual message. The language I quoted is Lodge's from the *Congressional Record*. The full letter can be viewed at http://www.presidency.ucsb .edu/ws/index.php?pid=65819 and contains slightly different language (although the meaning is very similar).

14. The full text of this letter to Benjamin Rush, dated December 20, 1801, can be found at founders.archives.gov.

15. In a situation similar to Cleveland's, Wilson's opponents might have argued that he was violating the Constitution. However, this would have represented a partisan attempt to stymie a rival rather than a commonly held norm. The public and the media were largely supportive of Wilson's move and saw it as a positive development.

16. Wilson's final two messages (1919, 1920) were written because of his failing health. Only Calvin Coolidge's first message (1923) was spoken, and all of Herbert Hoover's messages were written.

Chapter 5. Going National: Warren G. Harding
to George H. W. Bush, 1922–1992

1. An important caveat is the franchise was not truly universal until after 1965.

2. DW nominate scores are a measure of ideology that allows political scientists to conceptualize polarization in Congress.

3. The first in-car radios were manufactured in 1930, and FM was invented in 1933.

4. The percentage of households with radios can be found at census.gov.

5. For LBJ's address, see https://history.house.gov/Historical-Highlights /1951-2000/The-first-televised-evening-State-of-the-Union-Address/#:~:text =About%20this%20object%20On%20January,State%20of%20the%20Union%20 Address.

6. Tulis validates this hypothesis with the claim that only 7 percent of official rhetoric was addressed to the people in the nineteenth century, compared with 41 percent in the twentieth century (1987, 138–139). However, a closer examination of the evidence suggests that this claim is weak. Notably, Tulis "automatically" codes speeches that were broadcast as being addressed to the people. This heavily biases the data toward showing that post-radio presidents engaged in more popular rhetoric. This coding scheme also completely discounts the importance of newspapers in the nineteenth and early twentieth centuries as elements of popular communication. It is simply historically inaccurate.

Chapter 6. Going Targeted: William Clinton to
Donald J. Trump, 1993–2021

1. *Between Two Ferns* is a talk show on the Funny or Die network where the host and the guest trade barbs.

2. Trump was suspended from Twitter on January 8, 2021, for violating the company's terms of service; see https://blog.twitter.com/en_us/topics/company /2020/suspension.html.

3. One important caveat about Twitter is that other people can utilize the president's Twitter account. During Trump's presidency, it was well known that White House deputy chief of staff Dan Scavino used the president's account (Bump 2020). Of course, this is true for any form of social media, making a direct comparison to spoken or even written rhetoric from the past difficult.

4. The current state of political parties is characterized by strong partisanship but weak parties, particularly among the electorate. The parties are weak in the

sense that they have little ability to control nominations and messaging in the traditional sense. Ideology is mapped to a candidate rather than a party. In the age of strong parties, an individual had to work his or her way through party ranks, whereas now it is possible to use public and personal appeals to gain candidacy outside of that structure (e.g., Obama, Trump).

Conclusion

1. I am referring only to their legacies as adept communicators.

References

Abbott, P., L. Thompson, and M. Sarbaugh-Thompson. 2002. "The Social Construction of a Legitimate Presidency." *Studies in American Political Development* 16 (2): 208–230.

Adams, J., and W. Austin. 1798. *A Selection of the Patriotic Addresses, to the President of the United States—Together with the President's Answers.* Boston: Folsom.

Algeo, Matthew. 2011. *The President Is a Sick Man: Wherein the Supposedly Virtuous Grover Cleveland Survives a Secret Surgery at Sea and Vilifies the Courageous Newspaperman Who Dared Expose the Truth.* Chicago: Chicago Review Press.

Allen, Craig. 1993. *Eisenhower and the Mass Media: Peace, Prosperity, & Prime-Time TV.* Chapel Hill: University of North Carolina Press.

Anderson, Benedict. 2006. *Imagined Communities: Reflections on the Origin and Spread of Nationalism.* New York: Penguin Random House.

Anderson, D. G. 1988. "Power, Rhetoric, and the State: A Theory of Presidential Legitimacy." *Review of Politics* 50 (2): 198–214.

Appleton, J., W. Cutler, and J. K. Polk. 1986. *North for Union: John Appleton's Journal of a Tour to New England Made by President Polk in June and July 1847.* Nashville, TN: Vanderbilt University Press.

Arnold, Peri. 2009. *Remaking the Presidency: Roosevelt, Taft, and Wilson, 1901–1916.* Lawrence: University Press of Kansas.

Azari, Julia R. 2014. *Delivering the People's Message: The Changing Politics of the Presidential Mandate.* Ithaca, NY: Cornell University Press.

Baldasty, Gerald J. 1992. *The Commercialization of the News in the Nineteenth Century.* Madison: University of Wisconsin Press.

Baldasty, Gerald J., and J. B. Rutenbeck. 1988. "Money, Politics and Newspapers: The Business Environment of Press Partisanship in the Late 19th Century." *Journalism History* 15 (2): 60.

Baum, Matthew A. 2011. "Preaching to the Choir or Converting the Flock: Presidential Communication Strategies in the Age of Three Medias." In *iPolitics: Citizens, Elections, and Governing in the New Media Age*, edited by Richard Fox and Jennifer M. Ramos, 183–205. Cambridge: Cambridge University Press.

Baum, Matthew A., and Samuel Kernell. 1999. "Has Cable Ended the Golden Age of Presidential Television?" *American Political Science Review* 1:99–114.

Baum, Matthew A., and Samuel Kernell. 2006. "How Cable Ended the Golden Age of Presidential Television: From 1969–2006." In *The Principles and Practice of American Politics*, 311–326. Washington, DC: Congressional Quarterly Press.

Baur, John E. 1955. "A President Visits Los Angeles: Rutherford B. Hayes' Tour of 1880." *Historical Society of Southern California* 37 (1): 33–47.

Beasley, Vanessa. 2004. *You, the People: American National Identity in Presidential Rhetoric*. College Station: Texas A&M University Press.

Becker, Samuel L. 1961. "Presidential Power: The Influence of Broadcasting." *Quarterly Journal of Speech* 47 (1): 10–18.

Beeman, Richard. 2010. *Plain, Honest Men*. New York: Random House.

Berg, A. Scott. 2013. *Wilson*. New York: Simon & Schuster.

Bimes, Terri. 2009. "Understanding the Rhetorical Presidency." In *The Oxford Handbook of the American Presidency*, edited by George C. Edwards III and William G. Howell, 208–231. Oxford: Oxford University Press.

Bimes, Terri, and Quinn Mulroy. 2004. "The Rise and Decline of Presidential Populism." *Studies in American Political Development* 18:136–159.

Biser, Margaret. 2016. "The Fireside Chats: Roosevelt's Radio Talks; the White House Speaks to America." White House Historical Association. https://www.whitehousehistory.org/the-fireside-chats-roosevelts-radio-talks.

Braden, Waldo W., and Earnest Brandenburg. 1955. "Roosevelt's Fireside Chats." *Speech Monographs* 22 (5): 290–302.

Brookhiser, R. 2011. *James Madison*. Phoenix, AZ: Basic Books.

Browne, Stephen Howard. 2008. "Andrew Johnson and the Politics of Character." In *Before the Rhetorical Presidency*, edited by Martin Medhurst, 194–212. College Station: Texas A&M University Press.

Bulla, D. W. 2009. "Abraham Lincoln and Press Suppression Reconsidered." *American Journalism* 26 (4): 11–33.

Bump, Philip. 2020. "How Much of Trump's Presidency Has He Spent Tweeting?" *Washington Post*. May 12. https://www.washingtonpost.com/politics/2020/05/12/how-much-trumps-presidency-has-he-spent-tweeting/.

Calhoun, Charles W. 2006. *Conceiving a New Republic: The Republican Party and the Southern Question, 1869–1900*. Lawrence: University Press of Kansas.

Calhoun, Charles W. 2010. *From Bloody Shirt to Full Dinner Pail: The Transformation of Politics and Governance in the Gilded Age*. New York: Hill & Wang.

Campbell, Kathryn K., and Kathleen Hall Jamieson. 2008. *Presidents Creating the Presidency: Deeds Done in Words*. Chicago: University of Chicago Press.

Carcasson, M. 1998. "Herbert Hoover and the Presidential Campaign of 1932: The Failure of Apologia." *Presidential Studies Quarterly* 28 (2): 349–365.

Carroll, Raymond L. 1987. "The Inadvertent Radio Campaign of Harry S. Truman." *Journal of Broadcasting and Electronic Media* 31 (2): 119–132.

Ceaser, James, G. E. Thurow, Jeffrey Tulis, and J. M. Bessette. 1981. "The Rise of the Rhetorical Presidency." *Presidential Studies Quarterly* 11 (2): 158–171.

Chamberlain, I. 1856. *Biography of Millard Fillmore*. Buffalo, NY: Thomas & Lathrops.

Chernow, Ron. 2010. *Washington: A Life*. New York: Perigee/Penguin Publishing.

Chitwood, Oliver P. 1939. *John Tyler: Champion of the Old South*. New York: D. Appleton–Century.

Clements, Kendrick A. 1992. *The Presidency of Woodrow Wilson*. Lawrence: University Press of Kansas.

Coe, Kevin, and Rico Neumann. 2011. "The Major Addresses of Modern Presidents: Parameters of the Data Set." *Presidential Studies Quarterly* 4 (41): 727–751.

Cohen, Jeffrey E. 2008. *The Presidency in the Era of 24-Hour News*. Princeton, NJ: Princeton University Press.

Cole, Donald B. 2009. *Vindicating Andrew Jackson: The 1828 Election and the Rise of the Two-Party System*. Lawrence: University Press of Kansas.

Cook, Corey. 2002. "The Contemporary Presidency: The Permanence of the 'Permanent Campaign': George W. Bush's Public Presidency." *Presidential Studies Quarterly* 32 (4): 753–764.

Cornwell, Elmer E. 1957. "Coolidge and Presidential Leadership." *Public Opinion Quarterly* 21 (2): 265–278.

Cornwell, Elmer E. 1979. *Presidential Leadership of Public Opinion*. Westport, CT: Greenwood Press.

Craig, D. B. 2003. *Fireside Politics: Radio and Political Culture in the United States, 1920–1940*. Baltimore: Johns Hopkins University Press.

Crapol, Edward P. 2006. *John Tyler, the Accidental President*. Chapel Hill: University of North Carolina Press.

Crook, W. H., and Margarita Spalding Gerry. 1910. *Through Five Administrations: Reminiscences of Colonel William H. Crook, Body-guard to President Lincoln*. New York: Harper & Bros.

Cunningham, Noble, Jr. 2001. *The Inaugural Addresses of President Thomas Jefferson, 1801 and 1805.* Columbia: University of Missouri Press.

Davison, Kenneth E. 1972. *The Presidency of Rutherford B. Hayes.* Westport, CT: Greenwood Press.

Deacon, Kristine. 2011. "On the Road with Rutherford B. Hayes: Oregon's First Presidential Visit, 1880." *Oregon Historical Quarterly* 112 (2): 170–193.

Depew, Chauncey M. 1889. "Reminiscences of Chauncey M. Depew." In *Reminiscences of Abraham Lincoln by Distinguished Men of His Time*, 425–438. New York: North American Review.

De Santis, Vincent P. 1955. "Benjamin Harrison and the Republican Party in the South, 1889–1893." *Indiana Magazine of History*, 279–302.

Dewey, Caitlin. 2014. "A Quick Guide to 'Between Two Ferns,' the Galifianakis Comedy that Featured Obama." *Washington Post.* March 11. https://www.washingtonpost.com/news/arts-and-entertainment/wp/2014/03/11/a-quick-guide-to-between-two-ferns-the-galifianakis-comedy-that-featured-obama/.

Dinnerstein, L. 1962. "The Accession of John Tyler to the Presidency." *Virginia Magazine of History and Biography* 70 (4): 447–458.

Dorsey, Leroy G., ed. 2002. *The Presidency and Rhetorical Leadership.* College Station: Texas A&M University Press.

Edwards, G. C. 2007. "Limits of Presidential Persuasion." In *The Values of Presidential Leadership*, edited by T. L. Price and T. J. Wren, 85–118. New York: Palgrave Macmillan.

Edwards, George. 2006. *On Deaf Ears: The Limits of the Bully Pulpit.* New Haven, CT: Yale University Press.

Edwards, George. 2009. *The Strategic President: Persuasion and Opportunity in Presidential Leadership.* Princeton, NJ: Princeton University Press.

Edwards, Richard, ed. 1878. *Our President's Tour South Embracing the Brilliant, Speeches, Receptions and Banquets.* Louisville, KY: R. Edwards.

Eisenhower, John S. 2008. *Zachary Taylor.* Vol. 12 of The American Presidents Series. *The 12th President, 1849–1850.* New York: Macmillan.

Ellis, Joseph. 2001. *Passionate Sage: The Character and Legacy of John Adams.* New York: W. W. Norton.

Ellis, Joseph. 2004. *His Excellency: George Washington.* New York: Alfred A. Knopf.

Ellis, Richard J., ed. 1998. *Speaking to the People: The Rhetorical Presidency in Historical Perspective.* Amherst: University of Massachusetts Press.

Ellis, Richard J. 2008. *Presidential Travel: The Journey from George Washington to George W. Bush.* Lawrence: University Press of Kansas.

Ellis, Richard J., and Alexis Walker. 2007. "Policy Speech in the Nineteenth Century Rhetorical Presidency: The Case of Zachary Taylor 1849 Tour." *Presidential Studies Quarterly* 37 (2): 248–269.

Elperin, Juliet. 2016. "Remember When Zach Galifianakis Asked Obama about Being the Last Black President?" *Washington Post.* August 16. https://www.washingtonpost.com/graphics/national/obama-legacy/funny-or-die-video-history.html.

Elving, R. 2013. "The President, Congress, and the Media." In *Rivals for Power: Presidential-Congressional Relations,* edited by James Thurber, 155–178. New York: Rowan Littlefield Publishers.

Erickson, Paul D. 1985. *Reagan Speaks: The Making of an American Myth.* New York: New York University Press.

Ericson, David F. 1997. "Presidential Inaugural Addresses and American Political Culture." *Presidential Studies Quarterly* 27 (4): 727–744.

Eshbaugh-Soha, Matthew. 2015. "Presidential Agenda-Setting of Traditional and Nontraditional News Media." *Political Communication,* 1–20.

Eshbaugh-Soha, Matthew, and Jeffrey S. Peake. 2006. "The Contemporary Presidency: Going Local to Reform Social Security." *Presidential Studies Quarterly* 36 (4): 689–704.

Eshbaugh-Soha, Matthew, and Jeffrey S. Peake. 2011. *Breaking through the Noise: Presidential Leadership, Public Opinion, and the News Media.* Redwood City, CA: Stanford University Press.

Estes, Todd. 2001. "The Art of Presidential Leadership: George Washington and the Jay Treaty." *Virginia Magazine of History and Biography* 109 (2): 127–158.

Feller, D. 2008. "Andrew Jackson versus the Senate." In *Congress and the Emergence of Sectionalism: From the Missouri Compromise to the Age of Jackson,* edited by P. Finkelman and D. R. Kennon, 258–282. Athens: Ohio University Press.

Ferling, J. 2009. *The Ascent of George Washington: The Hidden Political Genius of an American Icon.* New York: Tantor Media.

Flesch, R. 1948. "A New Readability Yardstick." *Journal of Applied Psychology* 32 (3): 221.

Frantz, Edward O. 2002. "Goin' Dixie: Republican Presidential Tours of the South, 1877–1933." Doctoral diss., University of Wisconsin.

Frantz, Edward O. 2011. *The Door of Hope: Republican Presidents and the First Southern Strategy, 1877–1933.* Gainesville: University Press of Florida.

Furstenberg, F. 2006. *In the Name of the Father: Washington's Legacy, Slavery, and the Making of a Nation.* New York: Penguin Books.

Gallagher, Thomas. 2017. "President-Elect Trump: Is the Past Prologue?" *Society* 54 (1): 10–13.

Galvin, Daniel, and Colleen Shogun. 2004. "Presidential Politicization and Centralization across the Modern-Traditional Divide." *Polity* 36 (3): 477–504.

Gamm, Gerald, and Renee M. Smith. 1998. "Presidents, Parties and the Public: Evolving Patterns of Interaction, 1877–1929." In *Speaking to the People: The Rhetorical Presidency in Historical Perspective*, edited by Richard J. Ellis, 87–111. Amherst: University of Massachusetts Press.

Genovese, Michael. 2006. "Is the Presidency Dangerous to Democracy?" In *The Presidency and the Challenges of American Democracy*, edited by M. G. Han, 1–22. New York: Palgrave Macmillan.

Gergen, David. 2001. *Eyewitness to Power: The Essence of Leadership from Nixon to Clinton*. New York: Simon & Schuster.

Gilbert, Robert E. 1986. "The Eisenhower Campaign of 1952: War Hero as Television Candidate." *Political Communication* 3 (3): 293–311.

Goodwin, Doris K. 2013. *The Bully Pulpit: Theodore Roosevelt, William Howard Taft, and the Golden Age of Journalism*. New York: Simon & Schuster.

Gould, Lewis L. 1982. *The Spanish-American War*. Lawrence: University Press of Kansas.

Gould, Lewis L. 1991. *The Presidency of Theodore Roosevelt*. Lawrence: University Press of Kansas.

Gramling, Oliver. 1940. *AP: The Story of the News*. New York: Farrar & Rinehart.

Greenstein, Fred E. 2009. *The Presidential Difference: Leadership Styles from FDR to Obama*. Princeton, NJ: Princeton University Press.

Hamilton, H. 1951. *Zachary Taylor: Solider in the White House*. Indianapolis: Bobbs-Merrill.

Hamilton, James T. 2006. *All the News That's Fit to Sell: How the Market Transforms Information into News*. Princeton, NJ: Princeton University Press.

Hayes, Rutherford B. 1922. *Diary and Letters of Rutherford Birchard Hayes: Nineteenth President of the United States*. Vol. 1. New York: Kraus Reprint Company.

Heith, Diane J. 2015. *Presidential Road Show: Public Leadership in an Era of Party Polarization and Media Fragmentation*. New York: Routledge.

Hemmer, Nicole. 2016. *Messengers of the Right: Conservative Media and the Transformation of American Politics*. Philadelphia: University of Pennsylvania Press.

Henderson, A. 1923. *Washington's Southern Tour, 1791*. Boston: Houghton Mifflin.

Hertsgaard, Mark. 1988. *On Bended Knee: The Press and the Reagan Presidency*. New York: Farrar, Straus & Giroux.

Hildreth, R. 1879. *The History of the United States.* Vol. 4. New York: Harper Brothers.

Hoffman, Karen. 2002. "'Going Public' in the Nineteenth Century: Grover Cleveland's Repeal of the Sherman Silver Purchase Act." *Rhetoric and Public Affairs* 5 (1): 57–77.

Hoffman, Karen. 2010. *Popular Leadership in the Presidency: Origins and Practice.* New York: Lexington Books.

Holt, M. 2003. *The Rise and Fall of the American Whig Party: Jacksonian Politics and the Onset of the Civil War.* Oxford: Oxford University Press.

Holzer, H. 2014. *The War for Public Opinion: Lincoln and the Power of the Press.* New York: Simon & Schuster.

Hoogenboom, Ari. 1995. *Rutherford B. Hayes: Warrior and President.* Lawrence: University Press of Kansas.

Howe, George F. 1934. *Chester A. Arthur: A Quarter-Century of Machine Politics.* New York: Dodd, Mead and Company.

Kernell, Samuel. (1986) 1997. *Going Public: New Strategies of Presidential Leadership.* 2nd ed. Washington, DC: CQ Press.

Ketcham, Ralph. 2003. *The Anti-Federalist Papers and the Constitutional Convention.* London: Signet Classics.

King, Elliot, and Michael Schudson. 1995. "The Press and the Illusion of Public Opinion: The Strange Case of Ronald Reagan's 'Popularity.'" In *Public Opinion and the Communication of Consent*, edited by Theodore L. Glasser and Charles T. Salmon, 132–155. New York: Guilford Press.

Klinghard, Daniel. 2010. *The Nationalization of American Political Parties, 1880–1896.* Cambridge: Cambridge University Press.

Korzi, Michael J. 2004. *A Seat of Popular Leadership: The Presidency, Political Parties, and Democratic Government.* Amherst: University of Massachusetts Press.

Kumar, Martha J. 2005. "Source Material: Presidential Press Conferences; the Importance and Evolution of an Enduring Forum." *Presidential Studies Quarterly* 35 (1): 166–192.

Kumar, Martha J. 2010. "The Press Conferences of Calvin Coolidge: The Voice of the Man." In *2010 JFK Symposium.* Boston: JFK Presidential Library.

Kumar, Martha J. 2012. "Continuity and Change in White House Communications: President Obama Meets the Press." In *The Obama Presidency: Continuity and Change*, edited by Andrew Dowdle, Dirk C. van Raemdonck, and Robert Maranto, 103–118. New York: Routledge.

Kumar, Martha J. 2020. "Contemporary Presidency: Presidents Meet Reporters;

Is Donald Trump an Outlier among Recent Presidents?" *Presidential Studies Quarterly* 50 (1): 193–215.

Lanoue, David J. 1989. "The 'Teflon Factor': Ronald Reagan and Comparative Presidential Popularity." *Polity* 21 (3): 481–501.

Laracey, Mel. 2002. *Presidents and the People: The Partisan Story of Going Public.* College Station: Texas A&M University Press.

Laracey, Mel. 2008. "Talking without Speaking and Other Curiosities." In *Before the Rhetorical Presidency*, edited by Martin Medhurst, 18–28. College Station: Texas A&M University Press.

Laracey, Mel. 2021. *Informing a Nation: The Newspaper Presidency of Thomas Jefferson.* Ann Arbor: University of Michigan Press.

Lewis, Jeffrey B., Keith Poole, Howard Rosenthal, Adam Boche, Aaron Rudkin, and Luke Sonnet. 2022. *Voteview: Congressional Roll-Call Votes Database.* https://voteview.com/.

Lewis, Tom. 1992. "'A Godlike Presence': The Impact of Radio on the 1920s and 1930s." *OAH Magazine of History* 6 (4): 26–33.

Lim, Elvin. 2008. *The Anti-Intellectual Presidency: The Decline of Presidential Rhetoric from George Washington to George W. Bush.* Oxford: Oxford University Press.

Link, Arthur S. 2017. *Woodrow Wilson and a Revolutionary World, 1913–1921.* Chapel Hill: University of North Carolina Press.

Lowry, Edward, G. 1910. "One Year of Mr. Taft." *North American Review* 191 (652): 289–301.

Lowi, Theodore J. 1985. *The Personal President: Power Invested, Promise Unfulfilled.* Ithaca, NY: Cornell University Press.

Lucas, S. E. 2008. "Present at the Founding: The Rhetorical Presidency in Historical Perspective." In *Before the Rhetorical Presidency*, edited by Martin Medhurst, 35–41. College Station: Texas A&M University Press.

Lupel, A. 2001. "The Place of Sovereignty: Popular Power, Partisan Guardians, and the Legitimacy of the President." *Constellations* 8 (3): 304–312.

McDonald, Forrest. 1976. *The Presidency of Thomas Jefferson.* Lawrence: University Press of Kansas.

McDonald, Forrest. 1994. *The American Presidency: An Intellectual History.* Lawrence: University Press of Kansas.

Meacham, Jon. 2008. *American Lion: Andrew Jackson in the White House.* New York: Random House.

Meacham, Jon. 2012. *Thomas Jefferson: The Art of Power.* New York: Random House.

Medhurst, Martin, ed. 2008. *Before the Rhetorical Presidency*. College Station: Texas A&M University Press.

Moats, Sandra. 2010. *Celebrating the Republic: Presidential Ceremony and Popular Sovereignty, from Washington to Monroe*. De Kalb: Northern Illinois University Press.

Morgan, H. W. 1969. *From Hayes to McKinley: National Party Politics, 1877–1896*. Syracuse, NY: Syracuse University Press.

Muggeo, Vito M. 2008. "Segmented: An R Package to Fit Regression Models with Broken-Line Relationships." *R News* 8 (1): 20–25.

Nelson, W. Dale. 1998. *Who Speaks for the President? The White House Press Secretary from Cleveland to Clinton*. Syracuse, NY: Syracuse University Press.

Neustadt, Richard. (1960) 1991. *Presidential Power and the Modern Presidents: The Politics of Leadership from Roosevelt to Reagan*. New York: Simon & Schuster.

Nevins, Allan. 1962. *Grover Cleveland: A Study in Courage*. New York: Dodd Mead.

Nichols, David K. 1994. *The Myth of the Modern Presidency*. State College, PA: Penn State University Press.

O'Gorman, Ned. 2008. "Eisenhower and the American Sublime." *Quarterly Journal of Speech* 94 (1): 44–72.

Parsons, Lynn H. 2009. *The Birth of Modern Politics: Andrew Jackson, John Quincy Adams, and the Election of 1828*. Oxford: Oxford University Press.

Pasley, Jeffrey L. 2001. *The Tyranny of Printers: Newspaper Politics in the Early American Republic*. Charlottesville: University of Virginia.

Pasley, Jeffrey L. 2013. *The First Presidential Contest: 1796 and the Founding of American Democracy*. Lawrence: University Press of Kansas.

Pasley, Jeffrey L. 2015. "The Devolution of 1800: Jefferson's Election and the Birth of American Government." In *American at the Ballot Box: Elections and Political History*, edited by G. Davies and Julian E. Zeilzer, 13–35. Philadelphia: University of Pennsylvania Press.

Paul, Ezra. 1998. "Congressional Relations and 'Public Relations' in the Administration of Rutherford B. Hayes (1877–81)." *Presidential Studies Quarterly* 28 (1): 68–87.

Peters, Gerhard, and John T. Woolley. 2021. "The State of the Union, Background and Reference Table." In *The American Presidency Project*, edited by John T. Woolley and Gerhard Peters. Santa Barbara: University of California, 1999–2021. https://www.presidency.ucsb.edu/node/324107/.

Peterson, Norma L. 1989. *The Presidencies of William Henry Harrison and John Tyler*. Lawrence: University Press of Kansas.

Pew Research Center. 2014. *Political Polarization in the American Public: How Increasing Ideological Uniformity and Partisan Apathy Affect Politics, Compromise, and Everyday Life.* https://www.pewresearch.org/wp-content/uploads/sites/4/2014/06/6-12-2014-Political-Polarization-Release.pdf.

Phifer, G. 1952. "Andrew Johnson Takes a Trip." *Tennessee Historical Quarterly*, 3–22.

Pluta, Anne C. 2013. "The Evolution of Popular Presidential Communication." Diss., University of California–Santa Barbara.

Pluta, Anne C. 2014. "Presidential Politics on Tour from George Washington to Woodrow Wilson." *Congress and the Presidency* 41 (3): 335–361.

Pluta, Anne C. 2015. "Re-assessing the Assumptions behind the Evolution of Popular Presidential Communication." *Presidential Studies Quarterly* 45 (1): 70–90.

Pluta, Anne C. 2021. "Insecure Presidents: The Quest for Legitimacy and Innovation in Presidential Rhetoric." *Congress and the Presidency*, 1–23.

Pollard, J. E. 1947. *The Presidents and the Press.* New York: Macmillan.

Ponder, S. 1998. *Managing the Press: Origins of the Media Presidency, 1897–1933.* New York: Palgrave.

Prosper, Alan F. 1961. "'Silent Cal' Coolidge—Conversationalist Extraordinary." *Today's Speech* 9 (1): 6–33. https://doi.org/10.1080/01463376109385169.

Purcell, Richard J. 1936. "An Irish Crusader for American Democracy: Matt Lyon, 1750–1822." *Studies: An Irish Quarterly Review* 25: 47–64.

Quint, Harold H., and Robert H. Ferrell. 1964. *The Talkative President: The Off-the-Record Press Conferences of Calvin Coolidge.* New York: Garland Press.

Ragsdale, Lynn. 1984. "The Politics of Presidential Speechmaking, 1949–1980." *American Political Science Review* 78 (4): 971–984.

Ragsdale, Lynn. 1987. "Presidential Speechmaking and the Public Audience: Individual Presidents and Group Attitudes." *Journal of Politics* 49 (3): 704–736.

Ray, T. M. 1983. "Not One Cent for Tribute: The Public Addresses and American Popular Reaction to the XYZ Affair, 1798–1799." *Journal of the Early Republic* 3 (4): 389–412.

Rottinghaus, Brandon. 2010. *The Provisional Pulpit: The Modern Presidential Leadership of Public Opinion.* College Station: Texas A&M University Press.

Rutland, R. A. 1990. *The Presidency of James Madison.* Lawrence: University Press of Kansas.

Ryfe, David M. 1999. "Franklin Roosevelt and the Fireside Chats." *Journal of Communication*, 80–103.

Ryfe, David. 2005. *Presidents in Culture: The Meaning of Presidential Communication.* New York: Peter Lang.

Scacco, Joshua, and Kevin Coe. 2016. "The Ubiquitous Presidency: Toward a New Paradigm for Studying Presidential Communication." *International Journal of Communication* 10 (24): 2014–2037.

Scheele, Henry Z. 1989. "Response to the Kennedy Administration: The Joint Senate-House Republican Leadership Press Conferences." *Presidential Studies Quarterly* 19 (4): 825–846.

Schudson, M. 2001. "The Objectivity Norm in American Journalism." *Journalism* 2 (2): 149–170.

Simpson, Brooks D. 1998. *The Reconstruction Presidents.* Lawrence: University Press of Kansas.

Skowronek, Stephen. 1997. *The Politics Presidents Make: Leadership from John Adams to Bill Clinton.* Cambridge, MA: Harvard University Press.

Slagell, Amy R. 2008. "The Challenges of Reunification: Rutherford B. Hayes on the Close Race and the Racial Divide." In *Before the Rhetorical Presidency*, edited by Richard J. Ellis, 243–266. College Station: Texas A&M University Press.

Smith, Elbert B. 1975. *The Presidency of James Buchanan.* Lawrence: University Press of Kansas.

Smith, Elbert B. 1988. *The Presidencies of Zachary Taylor and Millard Fillmore.* Lawrence: University Press of Kansas.

Sobieraj, Sarah, and Jeffrey M. Berry. 2011. "From Incivility to Outrage: Political Discourse in Blogs, Talk Radio, and Cable News." *Political Communication* 28 (1): 19–41.

Spillman, Lynn. 1997. *Nation and Commemoration: Creating National Identities in the United States and Australia.* Cambridge: Cambridge University Press.

Stinchcombe, W. 1980. *The XYZ Affair.* New York: Greenwood Press.

Stolee, Galen, and Steve Canton. 2018. "Twitter, Trump, and the Base: A Shift to a New Form of Presidential Talk?" *Signs and Society* 6 (1): 147–165.

Stover, John F. 2008. *American Railroads.* Chicago: University of Chicago Press.

Stuckey, Mary. 1991. *The President as Interpreter-in-Chief.* Chatham, NJ: Chatham House.

Stuckey, Mary. 2018. *Political Vocabularies: FDR, the Clergy Letters, and the Elements of Political Argument.* Lansing: Michigan State University Press.

Sullivan, M. 1924. "Will Radio Make the People the Government." *Radio Broadcast* 6 (1): 19–25.

Summers, H. B. n.d. "Radio in the 1948 Campaign." *Quarterly Journal of Speech* 34 (4): 432–438.

Supplement to *The Congressional Globe.* 1868. *Containing the Proceedings of the Senate Sitting for the Trial of Andrew Johnson, President of the United States:*

Fortieth Congress, Second Session. Washington City: F. & J. Rives & G. A. Bailey.

Tebbel, John W. 1969. *The American Magazine: A Compact History.* New York: Hawthorn Books.

Tebbel, John W., and Sarah M. Watts. 1985. *The Press and the Presidency: From George Washington to Ronald Reagan.* Oxford: Oxford University Press.

Teten, Ryan L. 2003. "Evolution of the Modern Rhetorical Presidency: Presidential Presentation and Development of the State of the Union Address." *Presidential Studies Quarterly* 33 (2): 333–346.

Teten, Ryan L. 2008. "The Evolution of the Rhetorical Presidency and Getting Past the Traditional/Modern Divide." *Presidential Studies Quarterly* 38 (2): 312.

Tompkins, J. 1985. *Sensational Designs: The Cultural Work of American Fiction, 1790–1860.* New York: Oxford University Press.

Trefousse, Hans. 2002. *Rutherford B. Hayes.* New York: Times Books.

Tulis, Jeffrey. 1987. *The Rhetorical Presidency.* Princeton, NJ: Princeton University Press.

US Census. 1960. "Rail Transportation." Series Q1-152. *Historical Statistics of the United States, Colonial Times to 1957.* https://www2.census.gov/library/publications/1960/compendia/hist_stats_colonial-1957/hist_stats_colonial-1957-chQ.pdf.

US Census. 1971. "Radio and Television Stations, Sets Produced, and Households with Sets: 1921 to 1970." Series R 93-105. https://www.census.gov/history/pdf/1933-44radio.pdf.

Vazzano, F. P. 2006. "Rutherford B. Hayes and the Politics of Discord." *Historian* 68 (3): 519–540.

Waldo, Samuel P. 1819. *The Tour of James Monroe, President of the U.S. through the Northern & Eastern States in 1817, His Tour in the Year 1818; Together with a Sketch of His Life.* Hartford, CT: Silas Andrus.

Waldstreicher, David. 1997. *In the Midst of Perpetual Fetes: The Making of American Nationalism, 1776–1820.* Chapel Hill: University of North Carolina Press.

Wallace, Jerry L. 2008. *Calvin Coolidge: Our First Radio President.* Plymouth Notch, VT: Calvin Coolidge Memorial Foundation.

Watson, James E. 1936. *As I Knew Them: Memoirs of James Watson, Former United States Senator from Indiana.* Indianapolis: Bobbs-Merrill.

Watson, Mary A. 1994. *The Expanding Vista: American Television in the Kennedy Years.* Durham, NC: Duke University Press.

Wattenberg, Martin P. 2004. "The Changing Presidential Media Environment." *Presidential Studies Quarterly* 34 (3): 557–572.

Welles, Gideon. 1911. *The Diary of Gideon Wells*. New York: Houghton Mifflin.

White, R. 2011. *Railroaded: The Transcontinentals and the Making of Modern America*. New York: W. W. Norton.

Wiebe, R. H. 1967. *The Search for Order: 1877–1920*. New York: Hill & Wang.

Wilentz, Sean. 2006. *The Rise of American Democracy: Jefferson to Lincoln*. New York: W. W. Norton.

Williams, Bruce, and Michael X. Delli Carpini. 2011. *After the Broadcast News: Media Regimes, Democracy and the New Information Environment*. Cambridge: Cambridge University Press.

Williams, Charles Richard. 1914. *The Life of Rutherford Birchard Hayes*. Boston: Houghton Mifflin.

Wilson, Major L. 1984. *The Presidency of Martin Van Buren*. Lawrence: University Press of Kansas.

Young, Christopher J. 2014. "Serenading the President: John Adams, the XYZ Affair, and the 18th Century American Presidency." *Federal History* 6:108–122.

Young, Garry, and William B. Perkins. 2005. "Presidential Rhetoric, the Public Agenda, and the End of Presidential Television's 'Golden Age.'" *Journal of Politics* 67 (4): 1190–1205.

Zarefsky, David. 2002. "Always a Place for Rhetorical Leadership." In *The Presidency and Rhetorical Leadership*, edited by Leroy G. Dorsey, 20–41. College Station: Texas A&M University Press.

Zarefsky, David. 2008. "John Tyler and the Rhetoric of the Accidental Presidency." In *Before the Rhetorical Presidency*, edited by Richard J. Ellis, 63–83. College Station: Texas A&M University Press.

Zug, Charles U. 2018. "The Rhetorical Presidency Made Flesh: A Political Science Classic in the Age of Donald Trump." *Critical Review* 30 (3–4): 347–368.

Zug, Charles U. 2019. "Diagnosing the Blinding Effects of Trumpism: Rejoinder to Pluta." *Critical Review* 31 (2): 242–254.

Index

Adams, John, 33–36
Adams, John Quincy, 43, 58
Air Force One, 156
Albuquerque Evening Herald, 137
American Tract Society, 193n3
Anderson, Benedict, 6
annual message, 96, 156–157, 158–159. *See also specific presidents*
Appleton, John, 63
Arthur, Chester, 76, 101–103, 192–93n12
Article II (Constitution), 24–25

Bacon, Augustus, 133–134
Between Two Ferns, 165
Biddle, Nicholas, 52, 55
Biden, Joseph, 172–173
Botts, John Minor, 59
Bryan, William Jennings, 134–135
Buchanan, James, 64–66
Burr, Aaron, 39
Bush, George W., 163, 170

Calhoun, Charles W., 97
Calhoun, John C., 51
Chicago Tribune, 87, 115–116
Chinese Exclusion Act, 193n12
Citizen, 39
civil service reform, 92, 99–100
Civil War, 67
Clay, Henry, 53, 56, 59
Cleveland, Grover
   annual message of, 122, 156
   illness of, 193n1
   newspaper coverage regarding, 74
   presidency of, 101–103, 110–111

tariffs and, 193n13
   tours of, 76, 112
Cleveland Daily Leader, 86–87
Clinton, Bill, 165, 166–167, 170
communication, presidential
   dimensions of, 11–14
   finding, 16–18
   golden age of, 154–156
   incentives for, 6
   methodology and approach regarding, 14–15
   opportunistic, 176–177
   strategies regarding, 10–11
   technological innovations and, 175–176
   See also specific eras
Compromise of 1850, 65
Congress
   Andrew Jackson and, 56–57
   Andrew Johnson and, 79
   Benjamin Harrison and, 105
   constitutional power of, 7
   Franklin Roosevelt and, 152
   Grover Cleveland and, 110–111
   Herbert Hoover and, 148–149
   John Adams and, 33, 44
   polarization in, 140
   presidential correspondence with, 35
   Rutherford B. Hayes and, 94–96
   Theodore Roosevelt and, 135
   Thomas Jefferson and, 36, 38, 39, 44
   William McKinley and, 113, 115
   Woodrow Wilson and, 122, 123–125
Constitutional Convention, 23–24
Coolidge, Calvin, 26, 143–144, 145–148